Hate My Face:
The Struggle Between Young Black Men and Love

Charles "S.I.L.E.N.T.W.A.R." Crouch

Raleigh, North Carolina, USA

Hate My Face

© 2010 by SpeakLife Publishing

All rights reserved.

ISBN - 978-0-615-41993-0

No part of this book may be reproduced in any form or by any electronic or mechanical means including information storage and retrieval systems, without permission in writing from the author. The only exception is by a reviewer, who may quote short excerpts in a review.

Printed in the United States of America

Dedication

This book is dedicated to every one of my nephews: Josiah, Marquel, Dajuan Jr., Dominique, Anthony, Zachary, Marc Jr. (M.J.), Lil' Mike, Matthew, Jaysen Jr., Lewis, Leron, Cameron, Jaylil, DeAndre, and Cory. You will all grow up to be great and successful black men who will have a hand in making this world a more beautiful place to live. I love you.

To my grandmother Myrtle: You passed during the writing of this book. I remember our last conversation on the bench at the rest home. You told me that, "I'm old, and we ol' folk just know. I love you." I think I understand now. I know you are the reason I didn't break down and cry while I read a poem for you at your home-going. Thank you for being a source of strength even after you are gone. I love you granny.

Hate My Face

To my mother- in- law Althenia*:* Even though I only know you through pictures and talks with my wife, I feel like I have known you forever. On the day I said my vows to your daughter, I told everyone that the day you gave birth to her was the greatest day of my life. Thank you for molding her into the beautiful, strong woman she is today. I find it an honor to make up for every day she has cried. I will take care of her for you. I love you mom.

Table Of Contents

Introduction: ……………………………………………vi

Chapter One: The Baby Daddy Dilema………………….....1

Chapter Two: The Subliminal Glorification of Self-Hate….....41

Chapter Three: Cherishing Our Treasures…………………..84

Chapter Four: The Spiritual Divide……………………...129

Chapter Five: The Value of Self………………………….180

About The Author…………………………………….....252

Introduction

I write to evoke feelings. Bottom-line. Every poem, every verse, every lyric I write is meant to either express a personal feeling or to relate to someone else's feelings. As I bathed in a warm shower one morning getting ready to go to work *it* hit me, <u>Hate My Face.</u> I had long been bothered by the problem of young black men and the love-emotion element. It's almost as if we have disowned love or cast love off as some sort of poison to our manhood. As with any issue, the logical starting point is to figure out the origin of the problem. Having read many books, it would seem fitting to start this work of literature off with an onslaught of historical references dating back to slavery, however, I am choosing not to do that. I chose to take a more present day approach to this matter. "Hate My Face" is a literary mirror to those of us who sit back and watch our young black men waste their lives away try to achieve some sort of fallacious machismo status. Too often we grow callous and desensitized to the imagery and issues that are a direct reflection of why our beautiful young men are being deceived by this "real n*ggas don't cry" and, "we don't love them hoes" mentality. Be it the shortage of fathers in the home, negative Hollywood or "Hollyhood" images we are bombarded with on the TV and the radio, the lack of spiritual guidance in our communities and/or homes, the subliminal messages of "misogyny equals status," or simply the fact that we no longer have respect for love... we must understand that love is a key element that is casually left out of our collective book of resolutions. They are taught how to "ball." They are taught the art of hustling. They are taught what a nine-millimeter handgun will do to "haters." They are taught the insignificance of a black woman beyond their ability to fulfill their lusts. The list goes on. On a more positive note they are also taught trades, life skills, people skills, and workplace etiquette. Nevertheless, we forgot the most important element in the existence of a human being - love.

Hate My Face

WE HAVE TO TEACH OUR YOUNG MEN HOW TO LOVE AGAIN. I hate to say this but it needs to be said. We are allowing our young men to raise themselves, we are raising them, or we are letting other influences raise them as "niggas". I have said it many times before, "We are born as black men, We are *taught* to be "niggas." One of my biggest fears is that we are raising a generation of young black men who will be immune to love. Love encompasses a lot of elements: respect, adoration, patience, submission, humility, self-restraint, and a teachable spirit. As we all know, we see a shortage of these characteristics in our young men today. These young men, inevitably, grow to be older men. This lets me know that love has to be taught at an early age.

My eight-year-old nephew, Josiah, pretty much knows that when he and his uncle spend time together he will be greeted with a hug. He also knows that when we depart from each other I am going to kiss him on his forehead and tell him that I love him. He has grown accustomed to that since he was in diapers. I make a conscious effort to do that. It has become second nature in a sense. I want him to understand that it takes nothing away from his young masculinity to receive love from another man.

It wasn't until I was 26 years old that I recalled my stepfather telling me to my face that he loved me. Did I know he did? Yes. Did it make a world of difference when I heard the actual words uttered from his lips? Yes. We all know that love is an "action" word, however, when someone who has always been a part of your life utters it for the first time it revolutionizes a relationship. Imagine how many of our young men who have never heard the words, "I love you." Sure, they may have heard from someone who didn't really mean it or felt as if it was the right thing to say at that present moment. But imagine how their life could have been or CAN be, if they actually felt love or had been loved. My point is simple. There are too many young black men who are aimlessly existing (not living) throughout life who either never felt loved, never felt the need to love, been taught that love is non-existent, or don't feel that they deserve love.

Upon telling people about the book, the subtitle, "The Struggle between Young Black Men and Love," it instantly led them to believe that this was simply another novel about relationships between a black man and woman. Once I explained to them what the book was actually about, I noticed the collective look of surprise and somewhat confusion in their faces. This further validated the fact that this was a book that needed to be written. I have read several books that deal with the issues and challenges facing our young black men, but very few, if any, dealt with the "love" aspect in depth.

I wondered if this was an issue that we just simply left out, or if this is a subject that we are afraid to deal with. Could it be that the subject of black men and the love element is too taboo to be addressed even by accomplished authors and scholars? Nevertheless, I feel as if it is the most important element that is missing or seemingly missing in the development and progression of our future leaders and household heads.

It is my opinion, through observation, that we are raising young black men who want to maintain a childlike existence, a boy trapped in a man's body. An understanding of the love and spiritual element within a male is the key to his becoming a mature and upright adult.

I have grown tired of our young black men dying at the hands of each other. I am sick of black men looking at each other as enemies as opposed to allies. It bothers me to see a young black male being incarcerated as a result of some violent, senseless crime. Are we not tired of watching 'COPS', and other crime based shows on television where the majority of the show involves the death or criminal activity of a young black man? Have we become so desensitized to the music that glorifies the killing of our young brothers that it does not even remotely phase our spirits? Does it not bother us that so many of our young brothers are going back and forth to prison as if it is a Rite of Passage for our people? Is it now acceptable to degrade our sisters in our music videos as if they are faceless objects? Does it not bother us that we have grown so accustomed to our young black men being seen as the next "statistic" by the media that they have almost reverted back to the likes of three fifths of a human?

Love can change all of that.

It is imperative that this book be read with an open mind. I have always believed that shock value causes people to respond quickly. Some things I say may offend you, but one hears clearer when he or she is offended and will inevitably cause them to think.

I understand completely that this book may not make me a popular person to some people or groups. However, the sole purpose of this book is to develop a sense of understanding to this specific subject matter.

Simply put, I love my people. I want to see us grow even more than what we have at this point. Yet, in order for us to grow as a people, we have to deal with the men, first. In the Garden of Eden, even though Eve was first to partake of the forbidden fruit, God chastised Adam. Why? Adam (the man) was the one who God warned, not Eve. From the beginning of time, God ordained man to replenish the Earth, *with* the partnership of his wife.

I truly believe that if we could focus on getting our young black men to shoulder up their crosses and carry their people to the "Promised Land", we would see a much-needed change. This cannot happen, however, without them first getting a clear understanding of the power of love and spirituality.

To love is easy. We are God's children. Ultimately then, if God is love and we are His children, then love is a part of our character and nature. The challenge comes in when one tries to eliminate the roadblocks that hinder love from being exhibited and from blossoming. Thus, I have chosen to deal five key "love stranglers" that I feel are stagnating our men.

The Baby Daddy Dilemma speaks about the epidemic ravaging black communities, single parent homes and the absence of the black father in the home. In this chapter I also speak on the importance of strong men in our communities and the problems that come with "makeshift fathers."

The Subliminal Glorification of Self-Hate speaks strongly on a subject that is very dear to me; music, specifically hip-hop. Also in this chapter I touch on black-on-black crime in our communities as well.

The Spiritual Divide addresses the spiritual element that is missing in our young men. I talk a lot about the role the churches should play in their development, and also some of the problems I see portrayed in the church. It also dives into areas such as reading, sexuality, and the character of true men.

Cherishing Our Treasures emphasizes the role our women play in nurturing the love element in our young men. This chapter discusses the way our women are seen, how we allow our women to be seen, and also the Biblical and historical roles our women play. This will hopefully help our young men to view women differently, and to help them see how precious and important they are to us as black men.

The Value of Self deals with the way the young black man should view himself. It also addresses the historical demons that have plagued us collectively. Other topics include knowing who you are, separating yourself from what you used to be, and/or what statistics say you should be. This chapter goes deeply concerning learning to love who you see in the mirror and accepting who and what you are and recognizing your value on a spiritual level.

My prayer is that you hear my heart in this book and then devise both an internal and external plan to help develop love -based black men.

Hate My Face

Side note- *This book was written over a span of two years. There were periods when I did not write for months at a time. It was a grooming process. I never forced myself to write. As a matter of fact, when I began writing this book I was 32 years old, single, and still contemplating getting my degree. By the time I finished the book I was 34 years old, married, and in my second year of college. Therefore, if you read a portion where I referred to myself as being single and/or having no education beyond a high school diploma; it was because at that time that was my reality. Also, President Barack Obama was still a presidential candidate, and Michael Jackson was still alive. I have to mention this because I speak about these two individuals extensively in this book. I went through several different transitional periods during this writing, as you will see.*

1

The Baby Daddy Dilemma

I am choosing to start this book off speaking on the subject of fathers, or the lack thereof. The family is the nucleus of everything. The father is the foundation of the family. Without the father, a father figure, or an active father; things may fall apart at some point emotionally.

Let's begin with a verse.

"*I...remember the day as clear as May, Granny yelling, "J...pick up the phone" down the hallway. The hallway of*

Hate My Face

the hospital, I enter...she's about to give birth to my next chapter. Joy and laughter filled my face as I looked at, and touched his face. Much to say, now its 2008, and just to see my boy I gotta drive through 2 states. Your bull--- I can no longer take...coming out your mouth with child support I don't pay. Never understood the games you play...receipts to prove the support I gave. So, to you, I have nothing to say, I see the courts is the only way for J. to see a brighter day. There's no time to play, I'm on 85, on my way back to GA...I'm coming son." J. Wills, Try Again

Recently, a close friend of mine, J., decided to do a song that dealt with the strained relationships of a father and his son. On J's verse he dealt with the challenges he faced wanting to spend quality time with his son, while simultaneously battling with his son's mother about custody issues. I know J. to be a respectable young man full of integrity, wisdom, class, and a zeal for life. Here is a man who works hard every day to provide for a son he rarely sees. We have had many conversations concerning his trials with his son's mother, and his attempts to be a consistent figure in his son's life. Yet he has been innocently tossed into the stigma of being a "baby daddy." Unfortunately, until the hand of fate turns in J and his seed's favor, his son will have to suffer from the lack of a loving father's role in his life.

On my verse, I chose to deal with the virtually non-existent relationship I have with my biological father, with whom I happen to share my name.

On my verse I say this. *"As I trace it all back, I'm your twin identical...walk and talk like you...our grin is identical. But I ain't smiling...years of broken promises...never called you pops but I still gave you props. Now I must suffer as a man, why you don't want me I will never understand. Never comprehend why I can't hate you...Real talk, I still wanna emulate you."*

On my last birthday I turned 32 years old. I still hurt from my thoughts of what could have been between my biological father and I. Granted, God blessed me with a phenomenal stepfather (*whom I'd rather not refer to him as stepfather at this point in my life*) that taught me manhood, and how to BE a man. However, that hurt from not feeling wanted and loved from my biological father will plague me for quite some time, if not forever. Every boy needs a CONSISTENT (and positive) father or father figure in his life. For years I have heard women say that they are their son's mother and father. Of course, I am not belittling the black woman's ability to raise a son, but we have to understand that there are certain things that a boy needs imparted into him that can only be given by another man. It gives me such joy to watch my close friends impart wisdom and love into their young son's lives. It gives me even greater joy and sense of purpose that they allow me to do the same. They are the blessed ones. However, as we know, many young men are not as privileged.

Statistics say that in 1960 single parents headed 22% of African American homes. I will venture to say that women headed the majority of these homes. However, by the year 2000 that figure had almost doubled to a staggering 52% according to statistics. Let me clarify one thing before I go into this. I am totally aware that not all single parent homes headed by women are due to a father who chose not to stay. I believe that the majority of society tends to automatically blame the black men for the sad number of single parent homes. I, personally, have several friends who are victims of the "baby daddy" label due to no fault of their own. For whatever reason, it was less "stressful" or more conducive to the overall wellbeing of the child and to that man if he and the mother did not stay together. Inevitably, all parties will do their share of suffering. The case in which the father (sperm donor) willingly chooses not to participate in that child's life presents a more serious set of problems that may plague a child forever.

    I literally get sick to my stomach as I watch certain talk shows now. To be more specific, Maury Povich, whom, in my opinion, is exploiting the "baby daddy" dilemma down to its most demeaning level. I remember one show where this very young, very beautiful young sister was in search of her child's father. I recall a particular show where this young lady had over seven men tested and none of them; I repeat, none of them were the father of her child. As these men (and I use the term loosely) celebrated with a sense of relief, and proceeded to call this young lady every degrading name that has ever been used towards a woman, I began to grieve internally. I will admit that much of my grief was not for the woman. Let's be realistic, if you have to test seven different men to see who the father of your child is and none of them tests positive, I don't feel as if you are *morally* fit to raise a child in the first place. My grief was mostly channeled towards that innocent child. He or she was birthed into confusion from the start. The child was born a "guessing game" in a sense, and was not born a priority. The priority was to figure out which one the father was, and who the provider is *supposed* to be for this beautiful creation placed in the care of this mother and father. However, even at birth, the equation was flawed.

The Spiritual Realm

I am a strong believer that spirits attach themselves to children at young ages, even at birth. I also believe that because a child is so innocent and pure in its newborn stages, they are more aware of positive energy because newborns are not conscious of negativity. The adverse effect of this, however, is that newborns also become more aware when there is a lack of positive energy towards them because they have not come into the knowledge of evil. Keep in mind that I am no child psychologist. I have no *formal* education beyond a high school diploma. I merely speak, write and conjure up conclusions based on my heart, soul, and a realistic look at situations and life based on acquired knowledge, experience, spiritual wisdom, and observation. I said that to say this.

I firmly believe that a "loveless" man did not become that way overnight. He progressed, or better yet, regressed into a "loveless" child. In order for a child to truly be a "whole" child, his origin (the mother and father's relationship) must first be whole. In order for anything to be "whole" (spiritually speaking) there has to be a sense of love somewhere. For example, the foundation of marriage is love. Marriage is considered the most holy union before God and man. The root word of union is 'unit.' In order for something to truly be a 'unit,' it must first be whole. Have you ever heard of something being referred to as a "half unit?" Even if something is referred to as a "half *of* a unit" it is still considered to be somewhat incomplete. Only scientifically and mathematically speaking do two halves equal a whole. In order for something to be spiritually or emotionally whole, the forces that made that particular thing had to first be whole as two individual units. A physically whole man and a physically whole woman can create a physically whole child. Here again, this goes in the scientific realm dealing with genes and DNA. However, if there is an emotional break or separation, the two cannot create an "emotionally whole" child. A unit is never complete without 'wholeness.' It all ties together.

Wherever there is a lack of love or togetherness, somewhere you will find a broken unit. Whenever a child is born to anything less than a complete unit, that child is born with a strike against him or her. Not only are those children born with a strike against them, more importantly they are born with a strike against their soul, emotions, and mental soundness.

    Let's look at this from another angle. Let's say that a child is born with a physical ailment such as cancer or multiple sclerosis. Let's also assume that the child is born to a "whole" unit. This particular child's mother and father co-exist in a loving relationship where they collectively have cared for, raised, and loved this child since his birth. It is safe to say that this child will more than likely endure many outer struggles and pain as a result of his physical condition be it chemotherapy, surgeries, and physical therapies. However, because a child has always had a sense of being loved and cared for by a parental unit, he will rarely suffer emotional pain caused by his parents. Now let's look at another scenario. Imagine a physically healthy child who is born to a broken unit. More than likely this child lives a rather normal, *physical* life. Yet the child is broken on the inside. This child will harbor pain, hurt, feelings of rejection, and bitterness long before it is noticed. Inner suffering is far worse than outer suffering. How? More than likely, outer suffering will be caught so early that it only needs treatment. Unfortunately, inner suffering is usually caught so late that it requires rehabilitation. This is not to say that a child who is born to anything less than a complete unit is doomed for a defeated life. This merely says that any child who is born in this scenario will have some healing to do. It is inevitable. A child cannot be born into something that was shaped in incompleteness and expect to live a complete life. Any young man who is born without the presence of a father or father figure in his life, knowingly or unknowingly, will have a void that needs to be filled. This is even a greater void when the child knows that the rightful father has chosen not to involve himself in the life of that child. I have felt this pain firsthand.

"The Deeper Meaning of Baby Daddy"

I have always been big on word meanings, word origins, semantics, and the hidden meanings of words or terms. I do realize that this term is not always used in a negative manner. Many married people will use the term "baby momma or daddy" and are in healthy happy, complete family homes. It is used jokingly, or as a term of endearment.

Let's look at this term, "baby daddy." It seems that the emphasis on this term has always been put on the "daddy" part of this phrase. Rarely do we take the time to look into the "baby" part of it.

Baby daddy...

Usually when this term is referenced it is used to refer to a "dead beat" father or a "missing in action" father. Most often it is used as a clique term to describe a child's father who is not a consistent figure. Let's look at this from another perspective. Could it be that the deeper meaning behind this is something much, much more revealing? Think about this. Isn't it interesting that no matter how old a child gets, even if a teenager or older, we still refer to that father as the "baby" daddy? Could it be that because that child never had a daddy in its' life as a "baby" or an infant that part of the child refuses to grow past that stage because of an incomplete feeling? Thus, is a child always subconsciously labeled as that "daddy's baby" and that father being the "baby daddy?" It's amazing how you rarely hear some children referred to as my "young son's daddy" or "my teenager's daddy." More times than not, no matter how old they get, it is still their "baby's daddy." Here we see again where there is a break in the unit. Frequently a child will feel more complete when they are both momma and daddy's baby.

In essence, we have a society of "young man" babies and "grown" man babies walking around.

When a "baby" does not get what he wants or gets what he feels he deserves, or what he was deprived of, what does he do? He cries. He throws fits. He throws himself on the floor. He has a temper tantrum and acts out of his emotions. Babies are selfish at times, self-centered, and sometimes very violent. Why do they act out like this? THEY DO NOT KNOW HOW TO RELATE WHAT THEY ARE FEELING INSIDE. Think about it. Babies make a lot of noise, but quite often we do not know what is wrong. Thus, society has made its own pacifiers and "remedies." We call them Special Needs Classrooms and/or prisons.

While I was a teacher's assistant in a Special Needs classroom (which by the way were all males and only 2 of them were Caucasian), out of nine black males that were in the class, only 2 of the young men had a father in the home. I watched how these young men were literally pushed to the next grade level. They were tolerated, yet not accepted. They were isolated and put in a trailer away from the rest of the classrooms. It was almost a makeshift prison within that particular educational institution. These young men were literally being prepared for prison life in a sense. I have since heard that some of these young men are in youth detention centers, which saddens me deeply. Some, however, have gone on to graduate from high school, and go to college. I am not saying that every black man in these types of environments (prison) is innocent and does not deserve to be there. Society has laws and if these laws are broken they have to suffer the consequences. However, we have to understand that in some cases these particular men who derived from "broken" units are victims themselves.

"You Just Like Yo' Daddy"

According to statistics, African American adolescent boys are at more risk of developing low self-esteem when growing up with non-married parents. The article states, " In a two-parent home, the balance between the mother and the father's different socializing patterns may be what keeps the self esteem of both sexes (when there is a female child) relatively equal. Apparently, the absent father upsets this balance, when he leaves the young male child in a family environment in which less is expected from him, and, consequently, he may not develop the positive feelings of self esteem."

Before I proceed; let me clarify something.

I am a 34-year-old single black man with no children. Many people, sadly, consider me to be a "rare breed." I am no saint. I am not a virgin. I count it a blessing that I do not have children out of wedlock.

One of my biggest personal fears is that if I do have a child one day, I will re-enact what my biological father did. I have been blessed to never hear the words, "You just like yo' daddy," come from my mother in a negative connotation. I will admit that as far as inherited traits go, I am very much like my biological father. He is a musician. I am a musician. He has a very soft-spoken demeanor. I have a soft-spoken demeanor. He is an educator. I am an educator in a sense. I silently idolize my biological father somewhat. He is what society calls a relatively successful black man. He holds a Master's Degree and has a lengthy tenure as an educator. Often times I wonder if he looks at me as "less than," thus choosing not deal with me because I do not have the credentials he has. I battle with thoughts like this every single day and I am a grown man.

"Sticks and stones may break my bones, but words will never hurt me," is probably the most deceptive sayings we have in society. The Bible says that, *"Death and life are in the power of the tongue: and they that love it shall eat the fruit thereof."* (Proverbs 18:21) This presents a very powerful statement in relation to how a mother speaks to her son about her "baby daddy." One of the worst things a mother can do, besides speaking negatively about the child, is to speak negatively about the father in the presence of the child. To make matters worse, not only is she speaking negatively about the father, she is pronouncing a curse over that child's life unknowingly. Let's look at this. She says to the child, more than likely in some fit of anger (doubling the impact), "You **ARE** just like your daddy!" *"You are"*

denotes a present state of being. It indicates that at the very moment in time you **ARE** the personification of whatever is being referenced in that statement. In essence, what the mother is *really* saying is that, "You **ARE** your sorry father. You **ARE** his mistakes, his failures, his slothfulness, his downfalls, his laziness." With that life altering remark she has made her son guilty of a crime (in a sense) that he did not commit. At this point the child will begin to recollect every bad, derogatory thing that mother has ever said about the father and instantly embody that subconsciously. This is damaging to the child's psyche and self-esteem. Moreover, even if the statement is true, is it really the child's fault?

This child did not ask to be birthed into this world. He had no say-so in what his personality would be; whom he would look like, or which parent's character traits would dominate his life. Whatever bitterness, hatred, anger, or resentment a mother has with her "baby daddy" should never be taken out on that child. This confuses the child, hurts the child, and inevitably damages the child's self -

esteem. Think about the number of young men who go through life thinking that they are dumb, stupid, worthless, lazy and ugly because they were told that by a mother who was a part of a "broken unit." I have heard that if you hear something long enough, you will become that. Thus if a child constantly hears negative things he will live a negative existence.

Please read this next statement and let it soak in deep.

One of the greatest poisons to a young black child (boy or girl) is a bitter mother.

I have seen this time and time again where a young man is feeling the effects of a bitter mother's subliminal attacks against the father. I am speaking in reference to a situation where the son's father is willing to enthusiastically participate in his son's life, and be a real father to that child. I am speaking about the father who pays child support, contributes above that, buys things for his son, goes to visit him without causing any drama, avoiding drama with the mother at all costs and missing days out of work for court to get a fair custody agreement. There are plenty of good brothers out there who are more than willing to be there for their sons. However, they are dealing with the biggest roadblock ever - the bitter mother.

Webster's dictionary defines the word bitter as: intensely emotional, deeply felt, harshly reproachful, coldness or rawness, and expressive of severe pain, grief, or regret.

A bitter mother is quite possibly no better than a mother on drugs in some ways. It all affects the child negatively. They are harboring a deeper issue that plays out on those around them; specifically that child. A great majority of the decisions they make are in no way logical or sensible. This is much like a person on drugs. They are bringing pain to a person and are 100% aware of it but choose not to make the situation easier. They are hallucinogenic in a sense. For some strange reason, they feel like by punishing the father their past hurt is going to be soothed. One will never get peace within by causing another person chaos. It's almost if they are trying to get revenge over something that was not meant to be, and not necessarily a wrongdoing. One thing we have to understand is that even when something is not spiritually destined to be (a relationship between a man and a woman), that is not going to stop the natural process from happening. This is why there are so many unwed mothers and fathers. If two people are intimately involved and a child is the result of that meeting, God is not going to stop that child from being born simply because the relationship was never destined from the beginning. That is equivalent of God going against man's self-will, which is the only thing He will not touch. The Bible proves this time and time again. To add to that, I think some (and I put the emphasis on some) women think that just because a child is the result of that relationship, it automatically makes it a destined union. That is another misconception. It's called the cycle of creation. You will deal with what you do. I know this firsthand like everybody else. A child is the result of the natural process. I feel like, subconsciously, people have a hard time understanding that. A bitter mother will shower a child with gifts (even when they don't deserve them) in order to win favor with them so the child will not want to be with the father. The child will naturally want to stand under the waterfall of gifts, as opposed to the brick wall of discipline and correction from the loving father. A bitter mother will purposely try to make the father's life a living hell, which can eventually make the father not want to deal with either the son or the mother. A bitter mother will try to sabotage her child's father relationship with another woman simply for the fact that she is still upset over their breakup, even if it was 13 years ago (just an example). This is rooted in selfishness on the part of the mother. More than likely, every young boy is going to do whatever it takes to please his mother. Sadly, bitter mothers know this and use this as a strategy when dealing with animosity towards the child's father. This type of dilemma has to be dealt with. This is very damaging to the well-being of a young man. It subliminally teaches the boy that un-forgiveness is okay. It is very dangerous when a young man in subliminally taught to be unfavorable or lack respect towards a willing father. This young man could possibly grow into a man who finds it hard to accept love from someone who is sincerely trying to steer him down the right path.

During my years of counseling and mentoring I have encountered several boys who fit this criterion. It's foreign to them. They don't understand it when a man shows them love. The only consistent love they are used to receiving is the love of a woman. Thus, this type of behavior can ultimately lead to total distrust of men, and will have a young man feeling like any other man is an enemy to them. It brings about aggressive behavior towards other men and could lead to this young man losing his life, sadly, at an early age.

They Need Their Daddy

Seeing that I have discussed the dilemma of baby daddies where the mother is lacking in areas, I have to speak on the men. I remember doing a piece some time ago at my church for Father's Day. I will admit that I am a pretty bold speaker. I get it from my mother who is a powerful minister of the Gospel. Before I started my poem, I congratulated all the fathers in the congregation. I made it clear that I was only congratulating the fathers that deserved to be recognized. My pastor had previously asked all the fathers to stand to be recognized. When I got up (of course, no disrespect to my pastor) I told the men that some of them knew they should have remained seated. Some of them probably had not reached out to their kids in years. Fathers who have purposely decided not to play a role in the lives of their sons are greatly to blame for the failure of young black men to effectively function in society. I cannot count the amount of times I have had female friends request me to spend time with their sons just so they can have some sort of interaction with a positive male figure. I thank God for programs such as Big Brothers and Big

Sisters, and countless other male mentoring programs. They help, but that void will always be there.

Think about this next statement.

The absence of a deceased father will leave his son longing for *daddy* through memories. The absence of an incarcerated father will leave his son longing for *daddy*, yet expectant of his return. The absence of a living father will leave a longing for *daddy*, and feeling unwanted. Every child needs a father, but every boy wants his *daddy*. As I stated earlier, from time to time, I still hope for a consistent relationship with my biological father. I can honestly say that I feel no ill will towards him. My only question is; why? I still, often, relive the times we spent together. It's that feeling of, "Wow, this is the man partially responsible for my existence." I look like him, walk like him, and talk like him. Our mannerisms are very similar. I remember anxiously waiting by the phone expecting his call. I remember hearing him talk, and telling me how it was back in his heyday as a young musician. His voice, though I didn't hear it often, always held an element of authority when he spoke to me. Why? I simply knew that this was MY father speaking to me. He helped me get my first car. I remember when I had my 2nd accident in that car, and it was my fault. I called him very nervous, afraid of what he may say, considering I had wrecked it only months before. His words to me were, "Calm down. It's okay. These things happen." I instantly calmed down. I knew just by him saying that, everything would be okay. We would occasionally speak throughout the next few years. A few years would go by and then, somehow, we would hook back up. Each time I thought that *this* would be the time when we would reconnect, and it would be permanent. For some reason, it just never happened. I last spoke with my father seven years ago at my apartment, as a full grown man. Every time, I admit, I felt like a little kid, longing for that father-son relationship that never happened. I am blessed to say that my stepfather never had a problem with my biological father and me spending time together. I think he knows that I needed that in my life in order to grow. I think he probably knew I was hurt by the lack of consistency from my biological father, and tried to adjust accordingly. The relationship between my stepfather seemed to blossom once I got older and grew into a man.

As I stated in the introduction, it wasn't until my mid-20s that I actually remember hearing my stepfather tell me that he loved me. I knew he did, but hearing it did wonders for me. My stepfather is a disciplinarian. He had rules and we had to abide by them. He wasn't abusive at all. However, he believed in the "rod of correction." I never missed a meal. There were 4 kids in the home. We never went without heat, or water. He was a great provider for us. I know he loved us. Did I think he was too strict at times? Of course, what child doesn't? Sure, we didn't always get the designer clothes, but we never went without the necessities. I look back now and realize that the times I thought my stepfather was being unreasonable in his discipline helped me develop into the structured man I am today. Rarely do I go to sleep at night without having my clothes prepared for the morning. I never allow my apartment to get but so dirty. My pants are rarely without a sharp crease. To this day, if he says he's coming by to visit, I am sure to have my place squeaky clean, dusted, and my glass coffee table fingerprint free. It's my way of saying, "Pop, your lessons still resonate within me even after I am on my own." I can still call him to this day in my time of need and he will be there to support me. We laugh, joke a lot, and take rides in his custom van with no particular destination. He still gives me that fatherly wisdom that every man needs. I joke about how it was growing up under his disciplinary hand. I said all of that to say this.

Even though my stepfather and I have a wonderful relationship, and we have a true love and respect for each other, when my biological father is brought up, the quiet void in my soul speaks. I think about what could have been. I think about how far more musically advanced I would be had he been a consistent figure in my life. I, instantly, am reminded that I may not have been wanted. I wonder if he died would I sit with the family, or even be mentioned in the obituary as his eldest child. I wonder if he has heard that I am a spoken word artist, and if he would mysteriously show up at one of my performances. I still fantasize about us gigging together as father-son jazz musicians for the first time. Will he read this book and reach out to me? If he knows that I am not mad at him. I just still simply need him, and want to catch up. The sad thing is that there are millions of boys and men who share this exact same pain as I do. It is a silent pain mostly. This is the type of pain that is usually hidden by men and rears its head at the most inopportune times. I thank God that I have been blessed with the ability to forgive. Not everyone has that ability to do so as quickly as others do. This can result in resentment, and an inevitable lack of understanding love.

    I cannot, for the life of me, understand how a man can neglect his son. If it is a drama-free relationship between the child's mother and the father, how can a man just turn away from his son, his flesh, and his own blood?

In 1st Timothy 5:8 the Bible says this, *"But if any provide not for **his** own, and especially for those of his own house, he hath denied the faith, and is worse than an infidel."*

I put "his" in boldface to let you know that the Apostle Paul is specifically talking to men.

The book of Timothy is really one big long lesson from Paul to his protégé, Timothy. He is explaining the order of marriage, the church, and the family throughout the book.

An infidel is defined as someone who, basically, does not have faith. They do not believe, or they consistently question scripture. An infidel is not necessarily an atheist; however, this person is more towards believing that God is "not that important," if there is even a God.

I find it interesting that Paul would say a man who does not take care of his household (children) is worse than one who does not have faith. I think this is proof that God is definitely a family-oriented Being. God is basically saying, "If you do not take care of your children, you are worse than someone who questions My existence." I meditated on this scripture for quite a while, and never really got the meaning of it. This constant meditation lasted for about a day and a half. Then it all made sense.

Hebrews 11:6 says, "Without faith, it is impossible to please him (God)..."
This leads me to believe that a person who exercises faith pleases God. On the other hand, a person void of faith displeases God. In other words, a faithless person is deemed unpleasant to God. You would think this is basically saying that a man who does not take care of his children is simply displeasing to God. This is partially correct, but you have to read the *entire* scripture. It says that this person is *worse* than an infidel. God is saying that a man that does not take care of his children is worse than a person who does not have faith. That is not good. So the question then becomes, "Why would God equate not taking care of your children with being worse than a person who does not have faith?"
The answer is simple. It goes back to my analogy about broken units. Let me take the time here and just thank God

for revelation. I really had no idea, at first, why I chose to deal with broken units. However, now it all makes sense. If you ever notice in the Bible after Jesus healed someone on four different occasions, He says this, "Go thy way; thy faith has made thee whole." A whole family unit consists of God, man, woman, and child (if a child is involved). This means that God guides the man, man guides the woman, woman gives birth to, and guides the children under the authority, love, encouragement, and nurturing from the man, as directed by God. This is not a dictatorship, but more of a partnership when all parties are willing and submitted. As we see in these scriptures (Matthew 9:22, Matthew 14:36, Mark 5:34, Mark 10:52, Luke 8:48, Luke 17:19), wholeness, faith, and healing are synonymous. When Jesus said, "Thy *faith* hath made thee whole," He, in essence, is saying, "You are healed *and* whole." If this father is not following God's divine order of authority, and not taking care of his children, then the wholeness factor is flawed already. Now let's go back for a moment. Again, 1st Timothy 5:8 says that if a man does not take care of his children or his household then he is denied the faith, and he is worse than an infidel. Remember, an infidel is a person without faith. If faith, and wholeness (healing) go together, and this man has "denied the faith," then he has ultimately denied his family (son) their or his healing as well. So, not only has he denied himself healing, he has also jeopardized his family's healing as well. This then is what makes him *worse* than an infidel. Notice it did not say he is worse than the thief, the liar, the cheater, the adulterer, etc. These are sins of the flesh. It clearly states that he is worse than a person who does not have faith. He has denied healing to his family (son). This could mean emotional healing. This is why we have so many hurting young black men who act out. They are walking around inwardly scarred by the lack of love from their father; yielding them unhealed in their emotional realm.

Boys need the love of their father.

Instilling Beauty Within Them

I make it a point wherever I go and speak or lecture that the first thing I do is ask that the most beautiful young lady in the room stand to her feet. It never ceases to amaze me that there is always reluctance in the young ladies to stand up *first*. I do this for the young men as well. I consistently practice this exercise for a reason. After the young ladies and men stand, I ask them to remain standing and request that the parents in the audience look around to see if their child is standing. If a parent does not see his or her child standing, I boldly say, "There is something wrong." Of course, after that is said, I am not the most popular person in the room any more. However, I know that it is making that parent think, "I need to exhort my child more."

Children, as well as all people, need to know that they are special, loved, wanted, and needed. However, young men that grow up in single parent homes need to know this especially. Where there is a lack of love shown, a lack of exhortation for that young man, a lack of feeling appreciated, and a lack of positive words imparted into that child, he will suffer from low self-esteem. Probably, this child is already inwardly suffering from thoughts of being unwanted by his father. More than likely, he does not feel loved from merely the absence of his father. He does not need another blow to his soul that he has felt since birth. He needs to know, constantly, that he is loved, he is smart, he is handsome, he is important to someone else, he is special, and he IS NOT his father. If he does not know these things he will suffer from a lack of feeling loved. He will suffer from a lack of being able to express love. Inevitably, as he gets older, he will grow more and more callused to the concept of love. Love may become farfetched to him, thus leading to a lineage of "broken units."

Makeshift Fathers

As I stated earlier, every boy needs a father. In most cases, where there is not a father present in the home, the young man will "anoint" someone his father to merely fill the void. The sad thing about this is that mostly anyone will suffice. I was recently watching a documentary on gangs. When the young men were asked why they joined, the recurring answer was, "This was the only place I felt loved and accepted." This deeply bothered me because I know that deep down inside these young men knew that this was probably the worst alternative to a real father that they could have chosen. However, anything is better than nothing at all. The hopelessness with which they spoke was borderline depressing. It's almost as if they knew that they were doomed for prison or death. I thought, "These boys need some major love and direction from a FATHER." They were bright young men, too. Even though they spoke in their own vernacular, I could tell these were not dumb young men at all.

As I watched how they pledged allegiance their respective "sets" and "flags", I thought about how that same energy and devotion could have been given to something in a positive realm. Of course, I am not saying that all young men in gangs are fatherless. I am well aware that some young men who are involved in gang life have fathers in the home, and even fathers who may have gotten them into gangs initially. I am speaking only concerning the young men who involve themselves into associations like these who are without fathers. This is not only limited to gang activity. Young men may involve themselves into many other types of lifestyles that are hazardous. In some cases drugs fill the void, promiscuous sexual lifestyles fill the void, and/or violence fills the void, etc. These are the exact same things that a GOOD father will steer his child away from. However, when that young man is void a father or a positive father figure, he has no direction and will inevitably choose these things to appease his emptiness. These elements will inevitably give him a warped perception of love, having him think that they will give him some sort of inner fulfillment. As a result of this, they will serve as "the next best thing" until they eventually make him delusional, thinking that this is the epitome of fulfillment. Gangs, violence, drugs, and sexual promiscuity can eventually lead to the death. Ultimately, we will be experiencing another black male dying as a result of looking for love, yet never finding it.

The Conclusion

We will always have "baby daddies". I am not going to fool myself into thinking that one day all relationships will be that of a love story with a happy ending. I am a realist. However, I do think that if we made a more conscious effort to reach out and help rather than watch and point fingers we could make a difference. Every young man needs some type of father figure in his life. IT IS CRUCIAL TO THEIR OVERALL WELL BEING. Every young man needs to be loved by a FATHER. If a young man sees that another man can love him in a fatherly way, then he will know that he can love as well.

To any mother that may be denying her child's father the right to play a positive role in your son's life; stop. Please. Your son needs his father. Your son will suffer the *most* in the long run.

Hate My Face

To any man who may be reading this and you feel as if you fall into the "baby daddy" category willingly, the time is now my brother. Ask God to forgive you for being less than a father. He will instantly forgive you and give the necessary inner tools to become that father that your son needs you to be. Pray and ask God to touch the heart of that mother who blocking your right to be a father. He will do it. I promise. The season for restoration is now.

This verse from Ed OG and The Bulldog's song, "Be A Father To Your Child" sums it up nicely.

"You see, I hate when a brother makes a child and then denies it
Thinking that money is the answer so he buys it
A whole bunch of gifts and a lot of presents
It's not the presents, it's your presence and essence
Of being there and showing the baby that you care
Stop sittin' like a chair and having your baby wonder

where you are

Or who you are----fool, you are his daddy

Didn't act like you ain't cause that really makes me mad, G.

To see a mother and a baby suffer

I've had enough of brothers who don't love the

Fact that a baby brings joy into your life

You could still be called daddy if the mother's not your wife

Don't be scared, be prepared 'cause love is gonna getcha

It will always be your child even if she ain't witcha

So don't front on your child when it's your own

'Cause if you front now, then you'll regret it when it's grown

Be a father to your child

Put yourself in his position and see what you're done

But just keep in mind that you're somebody's son

How would you like it if your father was a stranger

And then tried to come into your life and tried to change

Hate My Face

The way your mother raised ya----now, wouldn't that amaze ya?
To be or not to be, that is the question
When you're wrong, you're wrong, it's time to make a correction
Harassin' the mother for being with another man
But if the brother man can do it better than you can, let him. Don't sweat him, duke
Let him do the job that you couldn't do.
You're claimin you was there, but not when she needed you
And now you wanna come around for a day or two?
It's never too late to correct your mistake
So get yourself together for your child's sake
And be a father to your child.."

2

The Subliminal Glorification of Self Hate:
The Devaluing of Life

"Let's sign Charlie Manson to a record deal, that dude would kill...literally...Sales through the roof, he straight murdering n*ggas in the booth. It's embarrassing, music then to music now...no comparison, as a result of a weak beef, all of my brothers are perishing. If you kill in every song, man something wrong with you...point blank...For stabbing and grabbing money from a corpse we anoint shanks. The sound booth stank, cause it got bodies rotting,

we did we progress to this point from picking cotton? Licking shots and kissing glocks like they the 2nd coming of Christ, Lucifer is worshipped when blacks is killed in the hour of chaos. MCs who pay homage to genocide is Nazi if you ask me, cats be having they own chalk to draw outlines on the sidewalk. I don't know what's gotten into us...some sort of Satanic antic that got us frantic about preserving life. And the sad thing is...I'm gone get dissed for this song...you aint gone never hear this truth when you turn your radio on..." Psycho Rap, S.I.L.E.N.T.W.A.R.

When Cassette Tapes Taught Us

"I got a letter from the government...the other day. I opened and read it, it said they were suckas."

"Thinking of a master plan...It aint nothing but sweat inside my hand..."

"Today's topic, self destruction, it really aint the rap audience that's buggin..."

"Loddi doddi, we like to party, we don't cause trouble, we don't bother nobody..."

"Once upon a time not long ago where people wore pajamas and lived life slow..."

If you ask any die hard hip-hop fan ages 30 and over to finish these verses, most of them would do so flawlessly. We remember it because it had meaning. It was fun. It was enlightening. Nobody died. Nobody murdered someone. Nobody was selling crack. The artists were true writers who thought about what they were saying, and took the listener into consideration. They told stories with meaning and a lesson. Even if it was as simple as, "let's just party and have fun without any trouble," that was the lesson.

Hate My Face

I have grown to the realization that I am now the bitter old dude that's like the "old" music. I have been told that I need to stop complaining, and just "get with the times." *This* is what's hot. According to popular opinion, rappers nowadays are keeping it real and telling what's going on in the hood. They tell you how oppressed we are in the hood, and what we have to do to survive. If this is so, then apparently we have to murder one another, drive fancy cars, rob niggas, rock ice, sell crack, pimp hoes, and then make a song about it. Thus, if this makes me a bitter old man because I refuse to accept this as real music, then hand me my cane and Geritol Complete tablets. I guess this is the chapter where I will play the role of the bitter old dude who sits and complains about how terrible music is nowadays, and how it influences our men to portray something that they are not. Possibly, I need to come to the realization that making music, repetitively, about taking the life of another black man simply for the sport of it is indeed simply, "What's hot." I need to accept that it is okay and that this is merely a "different" form of expressing one's self through art. I need to accept the fact that an album that speaks of blacks oppressing other blacks through dope dealing, robbery, and killing can be considered a classic with the likes of a "It Takes a Nation of Millions To Hold Us Back," or a "Paid in Full." I have to accept the fact that Rakim's teachings of knowledge of self, and Chuck D's teaching of black empowerment and equality have been replaced with stories of "slanging crack to survive," with absolutely no moral to the story at all.

I will be that old dude. I pray that you analyze this chapter as I bask in my elderly wisdom…Oh wait, I'm sorry, I'm hating. (insert laughter here)

Enjoy.

Only Entertainment?

Hip-hop is a type of god in a sense, whether we want to admit it or not. It was/is literally a makeshift bible for many young black men, including myself at one point (I insisted that people call me Chuck in middle school after hearing Chuck D. teach through music). Let me add to that that statement. If hip-hop is a god, in a sense, then "commercialized gangsta rap" is sort of a false god. It has some of the same characteristics and similarities as the true god, but is deceptive. It looks like it. It sounds a little like it. It wears the nice mask, but hides the ugly truth underneath. On the inside it is very deceiving and cunning. It has ulterior motives. We can say that commercialized gangsta rap would play the role of Rev. Jim Jones in a sense (no pun intended). I am very much a part of the hip-hop culture thus I dare not put hip-hop and 'gangsta' rap in the same category. I pride myself on being a fairly decent MC/rapper. Thus, as with any other venture, you periodically keep an eye and ear out for those who do what you do. It's a healthy way of keeping up with the "competition."

The other day while heading home from work I decided to listen to the radio, which is something I rarely do. I can only do it for so long. It literally bothers my soul.

Possibly, there is some faint glimmer of hope on the inside of me that believes that, one day, I will hear a breath of fresh air actually on mainstream radio. That particular day was evidently not the day. To my dismay, it seems to have gotten worse. On this particular song, there were about 4-5 different rappers. It seems that they each had their selective individual life of crime to glorify. No exaggeration. They did it vividly. I had to listen intently so I could make out their verses because it seemed that about every third or fourth word was censored.

    I took it upon myself to do a little studying of these lyrics on my own. I had originally planned to actually put the lyrics in this chapter, but I decided against it. I felt it would be a waste of paper. I went online and pulled up the lyrics to a few verses from
each rapper. Now, I will admit, the beat was hot, but the lyrics were just terrible. I didn't see the logic in what was being said. I understand embellishment a little, but this was ridiculous. It was everything from hoes, to choppas (guns),kilos of cocaine. The lyrics were spit as if these

elements were a regular part of these gentlemen's lives. They rhymed with passion and great detail about, basically, the exploitation of black life. I find it difficult to comprehend how an artist can lyrically express himself in such a reckless manner on a consistent basis, having no regard for what is being said and what it does to the perception of black people and our lifestyles as a whole. I understand that every verse written is not going to be happy-go-lucky. You have to have a balance in lyrical content. I heard Russell Simmons say in an interview (while referencing hip-hop music) that you can't have America without the red, white, and the *blue* (the blues). I have poetry that speaks of my anger, my pain, and my troubles. However, there is always some light at the end of the poetic tunnel. There is always some faint glimmer of hope far off in the distance.

It seems that we have come to a point where negativity is the new "gifted." It's almost as if the more destructive your wordplay is, the more glorified you are as an artist in hip-hop. The biggest dope dealer is now the dopest dealer of rhymes it seems. A few of my boys tend to rap like this. They are still my boys. I love them. I respect them as gifted artists. We collaborate together on tracks and they respect the fact that I don't get down like that on my songs. It's an understanding that we have. I don't compromise in my music. I may not agree with their lyrical approach to music at times, but I allow them to express themselves the way they feel. We often clash on this subject. They think I am extremist. I think they are limiting themselves. I don't deal with anyone who I think does not have the gift to be a poet (rapper), when they are claiming to. I just have low tolerance for a guy who thinks he is a dope MC and can't spit to save his life. My boys, however, happen to be some of the most clever and witty rappers I have heard. So I challenge them to write something credible every now and then. This is always where the conflict begins. In my opinion, rapping the way every other cat does is easy. It doesn't take much effort. I guess it wouldn't be as bad if the lyrical content was not so horrible, and the songs that I took the time to actually read the lyrics to prove this.

Here is my analysis of these particular rhymes.

These lyrics combined came to exactly 300 words. There were five different references to drug selling. Moreover, there was an astounding thirteen gun references, accompanied by six deaths threats. To break this down even further, this means that approximately every twelfth word was a gun reference, a murder destined to happen, or a dope reference. This is bothersome on many degrees.

These are our young black men saying these things to other young black men. Let me repeat that.

These are OUR young black men saying these things to other young black men.

Perhaps one of the most detrimental things a person can do is to have no respect for another person's life. To have no respect for someone else's life is to essentially not have respect for life in general; including one's own life. This is the epitome of subliminal self-hate. However, once a person records his or her voice over a beat, takes the time to strategically write eulogies over it for the WORLD to absorb, hear, and purchase, it becomes a glorification of that lyrical travesty.

    A few months ago as I viewed Black Entertainment Television's special, "Hip-Hop vs America," Master P. said something that was truly profound. He said, and I am paraphrasing, "Hip-Hop doesn't love itself anymore." This statement is 100%, unadulterated truth. Hip-Hop, indeed, does not love itself anymore.

Many of my poems and songs deal with the state of hip-hop. I vividly remember one of my favorite verses from a song called "Ready for Love." The verse says this, "I know that we are conscious of love, we love our blocks, we love our glocks, we love our money knots, but self-love we've evaded. They have rated us R for restricted love for self. Our hearts are conflicted for this wealth. Perhaps if everybody rapped about love for 365 days, could you imagine the change in our ways? Could you imagine the length of our days as black males? Yet the facts tell that we are number one of the list of homicides, and today another young black male died."

One day a good friend of mine, El, was conversing about the state of hip-hop. He said something that was sadly true. His words penetrated through me, "The only thing that has not been done in hip-hop is for a rapper to bring somebody else on stage and kill them right there." This is so true.

While watching C-Span the other day, I watched Dr. Jeffrey Ogbar speak on his book, "The Hip-Hop Revolution." He made a point that really coincides with the statement that El made. He mentioned how when jazz music first evolved people were in an uproar about it. It was labeled "bad" music in a sense. The same happened with rock and disco. Looking back on this we now see that this was just a result of the mindset of the culture at that time. Jazz is mainly known for its ability to relax the mind, and create an ambience of peace. Keep in mind, this was at the same time when women had to be fully clothed on TV.

Men and women were not allowed to sleep in the same bed on television shows (even if they were married. However, if we look at present day 'gangsta' rap, we could not come to that same assumption some 30 years from now. Granted, revered musicians such as Jimi Hendrix, Marvin Gaye, and Bob Marley had their own personal demons to deal with: however, I do not recall any of them threatening to kill a "n*gga" on any of their songs, besides Bob who killed a sheriff in self-defense (so the story goes). 30, 40, 50 years from now people will still say the same thing about gangsta rap that we are saying present day, "This is simply bad music." I would imagine that much of the hip-hop purists and analysts such as I have come to a realization that either hip-hop needs to grow up and mature really fast or it may very well be on its dying bed. How much worse can it get? There is no such thing as a "shock rapper" anymore. How much longer will it be before cats are making videos around caskets with a black body in it? Think about it.

It really cannot go any lower before it's no longer visible.

Hate My Face

Many people say that too much emphasis is put on hip-hop music, and it should not be to blame for what ails young black men. I partially agree with this. However, we have to understand that music cultivates entire generations in a sense. If you look at the 60's and 70's we had the onslaught of revolutionary music. It was music that revolved around social change for the Black race and all races. Marvin Gaye's, "What's Going On" is, hands down, probably the most important album in music history. The emotion, passion, intellect and grace that this man sang with are undeniable. There are many more albums that could be named but I do not want to stray off the subject and turn this chapter into the greatest albums recorded by black artists.

I have often said that I am fearful of what our generation, musically, will give as an offering for African American history twenty years from now. Let me tie this all together. According to the U.S. Department of Justice, in 2005, black males 18-24 years old had the highest homicide victimization rates. Their rates were more than double the rates for black males age 25 and older and four times the rates for black males 14-17 years old. Although much lower than the rates experienced in the late 1980's and early 1990's, rates for black males ages 18-24 remain higher in 2005 than in earlier periods.

Rapping colorfully, and skillfully in some cases I might add, about this exact thing does not help these statistics at all. Regardless of censorship, editing, and parental advisory stickers, our young black men listen to mental and spiritual poison for a great deal of their day.

The Spiritual Factor

Just as food is concerned, whatever is absorbed into one's being will play out physically. The ear-gate and eye-gate connect directly with one's spirit. If you hear negativity constantly you will become negativity. If you see negativity constantly you will become a negative person. There is NO way around it.

Hate My Face

Let me clear one thing up. I am not one of these so-called "rap critics" who just hear a verse from a song every 3 or 4 months and then go out and crush every hip-hop CD I can get my hands on. I live this. I write lyrics on paper just as these other guys do. I stand in front of a microphone and project my voice into a mixing console just as these other guys do. I write hooks, do adlibs, and create bridges just as these other guys do. The only difference is that I feel I may know a little more about the power of WORDS.

Think about this for a moment. Marvin Gaye was 32 years old when the classic, "What's Going On" was released in 1971.

The average rapper is between 20-30 years old.

Something went wrong in our mindsets over the past 30 plus years.

Recently I did quite a bit of studying on the effects of music as it relates to children and adolescents. One study indicated that at the simplest, most global level, people of all races generally listen to music because it provides a sense of pleasure. Another study suggests that a great deal of people listen to music simply to accompany their current mood. For example, if someone is sad, he or she will listen to a sad song. When one is happy he or she will listen to a more upbeat song. As a result of the affective power to produce some sort of result from music, when adolescents want to be in a certain mood, seek reinforcement for a certain mood, feel lonely, or seek distraction from their troubles; music tends to be the medium of choice to accomplish the task.

Speaking of black artists in general, I appreciate the gifts and talents of artists such as Chris Brown, Mario, and Sammie who keep their music relatively clean and listenable. Sadly, when I tried to list younger hip-hop artists who fit this category, I could not think of any. Not even with a few phone calls to some teenagers I know, or a search of the Internet. NONE. Everybody is a killer. Everybody is a gangster. Everybody is a drug kingpin. Everybody is a pimp. Everybody is a boss. What happened to the love element in hip-hop music? Phonte, one half of the NC based hip-hop group Little Brother, (one of the most intelligent and witty MCs I know) made a statement on a verse that was so true. He said, "Most cats rap about how they ain't even rappers." Lou Paradise, a fellow MC, made a statement similar in a song we collaborated on called "Just BEU". He says, "If you making so much money from selling dope get off the mic and go back to what you know." I am going to try my best not to turn this into a chapter about the "glory days" of hip-hop, but it is almost impossible to talk about the effect that hip-hop has on young people today as opposed to how it was when I came up. It almost seems that hip-hop music today is the complete antithesis of what it was in the late 80's and early 90's. It is an undeniable fact that music has a strong influence on young people, and people in general. That influence is heightened when the person relaying the specific message is more identifiable to you.

People who argue for "gangsta rap," who are mostly the artists themselves, or those profiting from it, often use the "Hollywood" defense. This states, "No one says anything about the violence in movies and television," This is partially correct. I am not saying that the Hollywood violence should be downplayed or given some sort of pass. However, what I am saying is that young people make a more personal connection with someone or something they can relate to more.

For example, nobody I grew up with in my neighborhood looked anything like Tony Montana (Scarface/Al Pacino.) He did not, in any way, exemplify my struggle. Of course, the riches, the money, and the wealth were intriguing but it seemed very farfetched. Scarface was merely the "drug dealer's idol" in a sense. He was the epitome of success as it related to cinematic presentations relating to the drug trade.

Many people say that there is no difference in the way music and movies should be viewed as far as "suspending your disbelief." I strongly disagree. Movies are supposed to be fictitious in nature unless it is some sort of biographic presentation such as Spike Lee's movie, X. This was an accurate account of Malcolm X's life, superbly portrayed by Denzel Washington. When we see movies like Alien vs. Predator, Transformers, and The Terminator, we know that this is solely meant for entertainment. Music, however, is far more realistic. Nobody knows when music was "created." The Bible speaks of musicians and minstrels. Music is an artistic form of expression about real life issues. It is an art in which the artist speaks from his heart and soul about a cause or a feeling coupled with his musical gifts. When a brother sings of love and/or heartbreak as a result of a woman, that is real talk. When Marvin Gaye sang, "Brother, brother there's far too many of you dying" or when Donny Hathaway sang, "Someday we'll all be free", these men were singing about real issues. Could you imagine Donny, Marvin, Bob Dylan, or James Brown saying in an interview, "Please do not take my music seriously, it's only entertainment." Imagine if no one actually took these messages of hope and change seriously? How can we, as a hip-hop generation, change the whole paradigm of music and set our lips to say, "Music should not be taken seriously." This is like Van Gogh, or Nikki Giovanni saying, "Do not take my art or my poetry seriously." We are lessening the value of music. We are taking the original premise of this powerful form of expression for selfish gain. However, in some interviews I have seen by some of these artists, they are saying that they "live" this or "This aint a game." So which one is it?

Fast forward to present day "gangsta rap..."

The reason why young black men have pledged such a devout allegiance to gangsta rap is because they see a reflection of themselves. The rappers walk like them, speak in the same dialect, have similar swaggers, more than likely share or have shared brethren pain, often come from the same cities, and sometimes they come from same neighborhoods. They have a certain respect for these individuals because they have achieved the impossible in a sense. They have "come up out the hood." Accompanied with that respect, however, is an almost unavoidable yearning to become that figure. This is the reason why we see the "cookie cutter" mentality and trend in gangsta rap. If you have heard one you have heard them all. It's a domino effect. If a gangsta rapper decides that wearing his pants down to his knees is gangsta, others will follow suit. This is called the power of influence.

 A great many of our young men who live by gangsta rap grew up in the projects, the bricks, the trap, the hood, etc. Day in and day out they are exposed to violence, the drug trade, black on black crime, and the struggles of being lower class. Their minds, from a young age, are trained to think poverty, despair, hopelessness, and barely making it. When a person is raised in a society such as this they are constantly looking for a way out of that environment. It is embedded into the human soul that if something is wrong it should be fixed or remedied.

I have often said that I have no problem identifying a problem as it relates to tales in rap music. However, when no solution (a positive one) is given, the artist is merely glorifying or praising that same problem. In other words, the artist is giving his stamp of approval on the setbacks of our people given to us by the government (in some cases). Talking about a problem but not giving a solution is useless chatter. Simply put, the problem is already evident; it's the solution that people seek. People don't seek the problem. Had Dr. Martin Luther King, Jr. and others only talked about civil rights but never organized bus boycotts, marches, and sit-ins, we would still be in the shape that we were in back then. Here is my point. We have rappers that are not only neglecting to rap about a solution to a widespread problem, they are thinking of ways to make the problem acceptable AND profitable. On top of that, they are vividly describing ways to kill off another black man in the process. This is terribly disheartening.

I have heard rappers say that there is more to talk about than the state of rap music. I agree. Also, there are several big name rappers who have charities, foundations, neighborhood rebuilding projects, and scholarship funds. That is wonderful and I applaud them for that. However, what are they saying to the soul, spirit, and minds of our young black men? Loveless lyrics, crime filled verses, murder laced rhymes (the murder of OTHER YOUNG BLACK MEN I might add) does FAR more damage to a young man than their charities will do good for them. If I make a derogatory statement about a homosexual there stands a case chance that could get prosecuted in some states. However, if I make a song about selling dope, pimping women, and killing another brother; nothing will be said. Moreover, I can become a millionaire, gain iconic status, get a reality show, get a shoe endorsement, get my own record label, start a clothing line, acquire movie roles, be on talk shows, get nominated for a Grammy or an American Music Award and, BECOME A ROLE MODEL FOR YOUR CHILDREN. I understand having business savvy, and I believe in black entrepreneurship. I am not knocking these guys for their success. I totally understand that these guys "get on," and bring a lot of people up with them. They give those who may not have had jobs before employment. That is the good side to all of this. However, my question remains. What about everyone else you are affecting?

I once heard a wise man say that once someone begins to follow you, you instantly become that person's leader whether you want to or not. I find it hard to fathom that rappers refuse to take responsibility for what they are saying. It is almost as if they have absolutely no conscience about the images they portray.

Question...

What's worse; a KKK member making a song with lyrics such as those mentioned earlier or a black man? The answer? A BLACK MAN. Why? We should expect for a Klan member to that. This is their mode of operation and purpose for organizing and rallying, etc. The KKK's sole purpose is to make their hatred of blacks, homosexuals, and Jews known to the multitude. Young black culture has grown so accustomed to black on black crime in our music that it does not even remotely faze us anymore. It is almost to a point that if you are not talking about it then you are in the "minority", or you are looked at as "eclectic" or, God forbid, extreme.

This next statement will probably stir a lot of controversy.

There are times I wish that white artists would begin to make songs like this just to see the reaction from black America. Could gangsta rappers who sing these sorts of lyrics get upset? Would they have a legitimate reason to protest? If hip-hop radio were to heavily promote a "Michael Richards" of rap could we really say that what he is doing is wrong without having a "teapot" complex? Of course I am not condoning this; however, it is a mere slice of thought to be taken in. We have virtually become the musical Neo-Nazi Skinheads of our people. There is no middle ground. We rap about killing "niggers," while they talk about it. What's the difference? Is it because they are white? If that were the case then all black on black crime would be legal. If it is okay for a black person to speak on killing another black person, then it is okay for a black person to kill another black person. Think about it, because it's okay so long as we are doing it to each other, right? It's a different extreme but the exact same scenario.

It has to be said.

Gangsta rap is MUCH to blame for the "loveless" factor in some of our young black men.

They do not need another song about diamonds in someone's mouth. They do not need another line about the size of the wound that a rapper's "chopper" will put into another black man's dome. They do not need another verse about the scientific and mathematics process on how to properly cook crack (yes there are songs dedicated to that). They do not need another chorus about pimping a woman (which I will deal with in another chapter). They do not need another hook about the size of one's rims on his whip. They do not need another bridge about the joys of hustling on the block. This is all POISON. I have no shame, no regret, and no remorse about saying that. It is utter foolishness and an artistic setback to our people.

It is sad to say, but it seems that much of gangsta rap is subliminally sending the message that black men are each other's enemy. We seem to literally hate one another now. The above verses clearly back this theory. Why must we continue on with this cycle? It seems as if we are upset with the wrong people. Of course if somebody were to try to hurt you or your family then you have the right to get upset. We're human. We experience all types of emotions. I understand that. If someone were to try to take sexual advantage of one of my nieces, I will venture to say that I would want to hurt that individual as well. I am not ignoring the fact that we have rights to get upset and violent, even in specific situations. However, when we can rhyme about splattering a nigga's brains simply because he mean-mugged us; there are some bigger issues to deal with.

We Need a Musical Resolution

"Let's Get Free," an album by hip-hop group Dead Prez, may be one of the most thought provoking hip-hop albums I have ever heard to date. It's apparent that these rappers (m1 and stic.man) are angry. However, they are angry at the *right* things. They are upset with the systemic racism oppressed upon our people. They are angry at the way police brutalize young black men and blacks in general. They ingeniously speak on the eating habits (which I am guilty of) of black people and how we kill ourselves slowly through our undisciplined diets. They speak on the racially biased educational curriculum that is misleading our young men. Pretty much, anything that you can think of that are some of the key elements in the oppression of blacks is touched on this album. Do I agree with everything that Dead Prez believes in? No. Do I share in all of their beliefs? No. Are these great young black minds with a message that needs to be heard as opposed to the run of the mill, "kill a nigga, get money" innuendo? YES. I'm not saying make a "kill a white man" song. I'm saying make a "kill the white man's image of us" song. I'm saying make a "kill the ignorance" song. Make a "kill the stereotype" song. It is so embarrassing to know that a white man can turn on the radio and hear a song made by a black man that references killing another black man. This gives him a further so-called right to label us "animals" in his mind. Have our young black men become so callous and insensitive that we honestly feel that this is the only way to express emotion about and to our culture? Why do we make entire songs about different ways to kill someone who looks just like us? Is money that important to us that we have totally stripped the value of black life from our artistic expressions?

Shed So Many Tears

I tend to think about that mother who lost her son to the hands of another black man. I think about that mother who cries every single day because she had to prematurely bury a destiny she gave birth to. I think about that mother who drives home from work after a full eight hours and holding back tears at her desk while staring at her deceased son's picture. I weep internally for that mother who has to walk by her son's room everyday, which is still adorned with his belongings as if she is imagining he is still there. It is a shame that that mother may be listening to the radio one day, or watching a video haphazardly and hears these lyrics that glorify the same way in which her child's life was taken. I wonder do these rappers think about that before penning these lyrics. Love will make you do that. Compassion will make you do that.

Unfortunately, these artists (and I use the term loosely) are subliminally teaching our young black men that love does not play a part in their life. In essence, if these young men feel as if it is acceptable, cool, or "gangsta" to be that hardcore that you don't even have to acknowledge love besides love for the fame, the money, the fortune, and the status, then we have a much greater issue to deal with.

As I am writing this, I know that somewhere there is a beautiful kid, who is full of destiny and purpose, intelligence, and ingenuity that is flawlessly reciting some gangsta lyrics, and is subconsciously embodying its' message and may, one day soon, live them out. Sadly, this will be another life sacrificed to the grave or to prison. Gangsta rap HAS to be held accountable for its contribution to the deteriorating state of our young black men. Somebody has to be bold enough to stand up and say, "This is not helping the morale of our young brothers." We need to build and support more positive artists who speaking truth, empowerment, and LOVE to our young men. The same way a child can be influenced by drug references, murder references, and gun references, he can be influenced by love, respect, dignity, and life giving references.

  I have often told young men to whom I have lectured or spoken to, "If you choose to dress like the trend; that's fine. However, make sure you have something on the inside of you that counteracts the stereotypes that you will be labeled with as a result of the way you dress." More than likely they will dress like what they see. However, it is our responsibility to make sure they have the soul, spirit, and minds of a king.

The sad reality of this is that this representation of hip-hop is the type that hip-hop purists, such as me and countless others, are upset about just as much as everyone else. There are so many hip-hop artists out there that are promoting positive messages. We have many that we are acquainted with such as Common, Mos Def, Talib Kweli, Lupe Fiasco, Rhymefest, Little Brother, etc. However, there are even many more that America has not been exposed to. A lot of these artists actually get more shine and exposure overseas than they do in their own country. It's a shame that places like Amsterdam, Tokyo, and the UK have a better appreciation for positive hip-hop than the country that hip-hop was actually birthed in.

I simply do not see the logic in the incessant negativity in gangsta rap. If the negativity had a means to an end then it would be understandable. I have come to grips with the fact that I may be considered a sellout for these statements. The sad part about it is that it will more than likely be the black critics who call me a sellout. I'm the sellout? I don't care about how much money a gangsta rapper makes, or how he or she can afford to get the family out of the projects. Who are you influencing and hurting or poisoning in the process? If you have been afforded the opportunity to get 10 kids through college, yet influence 100,000+ others to consider a life of crime because of your well thought out rhymes; what good have you really done in the grand scheme of things?

If a gangsta rapper can give me one good, positive, meaningful reason as to why they talk about killing another black man in their music...I will be silent. It takes just as much effort to influence a kid so he or she can be successful without being a felon. I don't understand the problem with that. I guess I never will.

Our beautiful young black men will not learn love through "Beef" DVDs. They will not learn through Top Ten video countdowns with at least seven of the videos consisting of money, drugs, and misogyny, and every other song on the radio persuading them to get money (by whatever means necessary). I guess my underlying concern in all of this is that I truly do not believe in my heart that every rapper that does this necessarily wants to. I cannot find it within myself to believe that we as black men have grown this cold towards one another. I believe that a lot of this has to do with the record companies, radio, and ultimately; money. I have listened to certain artists who make music like this in interviews speak with great intelligence, impeccable grammar, and passion towards life, yet turn around and make a song about "making the nine lick shots". Inevitably, a young man growing up in the hood will do whatever it takes to get of that depression. However, not every rapper that screams "hood born and raised" is truly that. On the flip side of that, not every rapper that is "hood born and raised" is screaming "murder, murder, murder" on the microphone either. Thus, it leaves us to wonder who really lives this and who doesn't. Nevertheless, I still feel like is has gotten extremely out of control.

It is our responsibility as adults and role models to tell them, "You do not have to resort to these means."

It is our responsibility to cut off the radio, the TV, and the movies.

It is our responsibility to teach them love, respect, and the beauty of black life. It is quite obvious that the gangsta rappers are not going to do it. I urge you to take a more introspective look/listen to what is being allowed into your child's mind and soul. It can persuade them to take wrong paths in life.

Finally, to the gangsta rappers who may be reading this; please stop. There is no other way to put it.

Stop. YOU ARE NOT HELPING THE DILEMMA. There is SO MUCH you can give. There is so much that you can offer. There is so much creativity on the inside of you that goes beyond a "choppa." You are so much more, artistically, than the sell of an ounce of cocaine, or a pimp, or a killer of the brothers. You hold the power in your voice to help cultivate young minds to be something positive and full of impact to our people. Why are you teaching them genocide? Be heard and revered as a voice of change, and LOVE.

It's not hard.

Less Love, More Crime

For the life of me I cannot figure out why I am so engulfed by real life crime shows on TV. One show I particularly watch on a consistent basis is A&E's show, "The First 48." This particular show highlights real life crimes (all murders), and how the detectives have 48 hours to try and solve the crime. They say that usually if a case is not solved within this specific time frame then it is becomes very difficult to solve it inevitably. I was talking to a very dear friend of mine and she asked me why I loved this show so much. I could not answer it. The reason why I could not answer the question is because I am literally heartbroken every time I watch the program. On every episode I have viewed thus far there has ALWAYS been a black male who has lost his life to another black male. A young black male has always been either the victim or the suspect. It never fails. Of course, I watch it because it is ultimately an intriguing program to watch. It is always interesting to see how the story unfolds as far as forensics and other elements are concerned. Sadly, a black male always loses his life and another young black is always whisked away in handcuffs as the credits roll. However, one particular episode bothered me very deeply. This was the scenario. A group of young black men had an altercation that was caught on a gas station's surveillance camera. The young man who ultimately became the victim of a homicide was clearly seen trying to avoid the altercation. The young man was shot to death. After investigation, questioning, following up on leads, etc., the suspect was eventually caught and brought into the local police station for questioning. After some intense interrogation the young man finally confessed to killing the victim. His reasoning for committing the murder was literally shocking. When asked why he killed the man, the suspect simply said these words, "I felt like he disrespected me the way he looked at me." Yes, you read right. That was his reason. A beautiful young black male was shot in cold blood simply for the way he looked at another young black male. His mother will grieve for the rest of her life because her son allegedly looked at someone the wrong way. If our young black men are dying over the way they look at someone, the way they are dressed, gang induction, a few dollars, some rims on a car, or a small time drug deal, then life has absolutely NO VALUE to these young men; none. When our social morale reaches this low and our young men become this desensitized to life, we are presented with a serious lack of love issue.

I could go on and on about the crime statistics but I am sure we are used to hearing them.

Our young men simply cannot afford to lose their lives because of the way they looked at another young black male. Life is too precious for that. We are dying at alarming rates. We are becoming an endangered species due to a subliminal "no love" creed we are upholding. Our young black men are pledging allegiance to the wrong things now. I was washing clothes the other day in my apartment complex's washroom facility and saw how someone spray-painted their respective gang affiliations all over the walls. They put the names of their gang and ended it with "fo' life." I started thinking how these kids were willing to die for this foolishness simply because they had nothing better to live for.

    Every human being wants something to live for. Now it seems like the tables have turned. Something happened. Young black men no longer want something to live for, they want something to die for. We feel the need to have some type of cause to fight for. It's embedded into us. We are bombarded with violence, drugs, and this macho image and if there is no alternative present, then that is what we will adapt to. It is imperative that our young black men are taught the beautiful value of life. I understand that the conditions of society and the poverty some of our families have to live may cause a great majority of our young brothers to not have the greatest appreciation of their "present" condition. However, once a young man understands just the mere value of having life alone will make them want to achieve more. One thing I feel I can honestly say that applies to everybody is that we all want tomorrow to be a little better than today was. Even if today was wonderful we hope that tomorrow will be even more wonderful. With that being said, we have to instill into our beautiful young black men that tomorrow is a gift within itself. To adopt this type of thinking, we have to input more love into our young men.

A former co-worker of mine, PaPa Cisse, told me something one day that will forever resonate in my spirit. He said, "When violence starts, the heart and mind stop." This leads me to think that when the heart and mind are going, the violence will cease. I know this statement is rather far-fetched. This nation was started through violence and strong-arming. However, that does mean our "nation" as black people has to continue to live under this same principle. We have become our own predator and prey. We kill each other. We hunt each other. Sure, the Willie Lynch Papers may have been a hoax (suggested by some historians), but the messages in them still hold true. We are pitted against each other like a pit-bull and a Rottweiler, fighting to the death and to the penal systems while corporate America CEO's who invest in the prison systems make a killing. I heard an older gentleman say that, sadly, one of the best businesses to start within the black community is a funeral home. The deaths of young black men are being capitalized on right under our noses.

I read a sad statistic that stated that prisons are built based on the amount of young black men who are failing the third grade. The system is waiting for us to self-destruct. Until our young black men, who will eventually become older black men, learn that violence only begets more violence, we will continue to see this tragedy everyday. I see clips on YouTube and other websites where our young beautiful young men are taping savage beatings of each other. Gangs are shown showcasing their firearms as if they were trophies. The body count now stands as some sort of status amongst our youth. It's disheartening. Where is the love among our young men? Our young men no longer can experience the innocence of youth anymore. They are forced to be men before they can be children.

The Inner Truth

Being a spoken word artist and lecturer, to mainly youth, I sit down and talk with these kids. Most of them do not want to be a statistic. None of them have dreams or fantasies of dying before their time. They want to live a long, prosperous life. However, if no one is instilling love in them they will follow the trends they see on a regular basis. I want to see our young black men live prosperous, healthy, enriched, and LONG lives. We have to fight for them. We have to teach them love for one another. They have to understand the death of only one black male equals a small percentage of death inside of all young black males. Bob Marley was asked after being shot twice at this home why he was choosing to go out on stage and perform. His

reply was, "The people who are trying to make the world a worse place never take a day off; so why should I?"
I choose to fight for what is right as well.

3

Cherishing Our Treasures

"There is nothing about you that I would overlook...even down to the simplest detail of the way your cold in your eyes is shaped in our mid-morning conversations about life. Everything about you screams divine...seems designs of you were strategic before time was shaped.

Bait of my soul's hook, but there is nothing fishy about you...I fully trust you.

If I "hieroglyphically" fluent I would draw pictures of you inside ghetto pyramids... fully clothed with a naked soul so my brothers can behold the depth of your original mold.

Hate My Face

Blame it on my mother. I just can't help but to worship your strength...the way you intuitively breach dishonest contracts before I immaturely sign our lives away...my today is only a tomorrow waiting to relive our yesterday again.

Never understood why now you downsized to a thong in a hip-hop hook, when it's seems only yesterday you were the subject of Donny Hathaway's sadness when you left him, and how he wept for your return.

Let me learn of thee, my sister. A wisdom like that of Nikki(Giovanni) and Sonia(Sanchez)...spiritually swapping the Song of Solomon through semi-second eye glances.

I am not afraid to tell you that without you I was without me.

I am not afraid to tell you that without you I was without me.

Without a she a he is not a complete me.

And I don't see how they don't understand this...How they just reprimand this, "Cherish our women" proclamation and I am hating in its most complex form.

I will be called a bitch for you.

I will be called soft for you.

I will be honored to wear the badge of punk nigga for the sake of your integrity.

Sister, it's all because of my love for you.

My love for the look in your eyes when you tell me about myself...

The look of "I don't care what you got as long as I got you" when I fantasize about sharing a non-existent wealth.

The excitement I get when I hear your heels strike the floor when you are entering the door after I haven't seen you all day. The way you recite old school rhymes word for word with me while listening to old school tapes.

These are the reasons why...

I will never disrespect you.

I will never degrade or exploit you.

Hate My Face

I will never call you out of your name...and I don't understand...how some dudes...don't get it.
I will always love you. I promise."

These are the words from a poem I wrote some time ago entitled "Never." Clearly it is an ode to black women. In this particular piece, I am expressing my love and respect for the queens that they are to me (as I have done in numerous poems.) However, I am also speaking on the disrespect factor that has seemed to become a "permissive misogyny" in a sense, as it relates to our young black men. I have always said that the earthly manifestation of Heaven to a black man is the black woman. I will live by this creed until the day I am laid to rest.

This chapter will deal with three key elements. These particular elements are as follows:

1. Why we have allowed our young men to so openly exploit our women.

2. How the respect for a black woman (and women in general) can profoundly deepen the love element in a young black man in all aspects of life.

3. The key role a woman plays in the uplifting of our young men.

Body without a Face

I love black women. Some men have a weakness for money. Some have a weakness for a sense of power. Drugs are some men's weakness. My weakness is black women. I have no problem admitting that.

I am not going to begin writing this chapter and have the reader under the assumption that I am some guy that does not look twice when I see a "shapely" sister. I am a man. We are creatures of sight. It's a fact. However, admiring a woman's beauty and exploiting that beauty are two totally different things.

Black women are too beautiful not to look twice in some instances. It's a historical beauty, however, that I reference in my poetry and music most of the time. It appears that in the media the black woman is now seen as a showpiece as opposed to a masterpiece. It's not a taboo occurrence in some of our art anymore. Black women are exploited to demonizing levels now.

Just as I mentioned in the previous chapter, it seems like just as our men are represented as dope boys, gangsters, pimps, and ballers in hip-hop; our women serve one purpose and one purpose only, to be our trophies. That's it. It is nothing more, nothing less.

Jill Scott, one of my favorite artists, said in one of her performance pieces entitled, "The Thickness", that women are being put in videos to dance around and shake it, and it has absolutely nothing to do with the content of the song. This is simply done to attract viewers yet does not make it acceptable.

"Sex sells but the effects yell to damsels that black tails subtract the use for brain cells...And that's so far from the truth; from the video to the booth we stealing innocence from the youth. My queens get seen as thonged out

mannequins, dancing then vanishing when it's time to put on pants again...and I'm panicking."

This is a verse from a song I wrote entitled, "A Tune to Atone." Here again it speaks of the way our sisters are treated, or are allowing themselves to be treated in the entertainment industry.

Black people are a very rhythmic people. We love to dance. It's in our blood. We are, by far, the most imitated race of people as far as the arts are concerned. Our music, rhythmic expressions, and dance moves have been copied, mimicked, and made adaptations of since the beginning of time. I recall my sister telling me about a trip to the Caribbean she and her husband took and how they witnessed the culture of dance there. She told me how seductively the women danced, yet how it was done in a very self-respectable manner. The men were not exploiting the women at all. They were allowed to freely express themselves through dance without being called a "freak." The women dance in a very seductive manner, but it has a respectable undertone in it that screams "culture and freedom" as opposed to "drop it like it's hot" and "shake it for this money."

I will admit I have been to a strip club in my life. I have to say this because I don't want to come off as self-righteous. I will even admit that, yes, I did like what I saw. As a matter of fact, I liked it a lot. I am just keeping it real. Again, I am a man. It would have bothered me more if I didn't like what I saw. Granted, I was younger then and have grown into a more mature man. This is not to say that men who attend strip clubs regularly are immature. It's some men's way of relaxing or unwinding. It could be one way of a man refraining from committing adultery on his wife. I have even heard of some married couples attending strip clubs together as a means of "foreplay." If it's your thing, then it's your thing. A Gentlemen's Club is for adults and that is what you like then it's just what you like. I can say that I will probably never go back and that is because of my personal moral beliefs as a Christian and simply for the fact that I just did not feel like I fit in that environment. Sure, my flesh (eyes) were pleased but my spirit was ultimately bothered. The reason why I brought up strip clubs is because I recall hearing a particular rapper say that if we rally against misogynist videos, then we should first rally against the strip clubs in our communities. This almost made sense until I thought about one thing. My nine-year-old nephew cannot get into a strip club. No matter how much money he has, he is not going to get past security and will probably be laughed at, and be considered too cute and innocent to get into such an establishment. However, he can easily pick up the remote control at home and see a watered down strip club on television.

There are several facets to this dilemma.

One truth is that these women are not forced to do what they do. Apparently, they see nothing wrong with it. If this is the case then these particular women should not feel as if I am addressing them. In actuality, I am not really addressing the women at all. They are of age to make decisions for themselves and how they choose to be depicted. If a black woman feels like shaking her posterior is her "calling", or if she feels that this is an avenue to get her to where she really wants to be in life, i.e., getting her through college, etc, then that is her choice. Some women may work 2 jobs. Some women may be a video girl or stripper. If they both end up being a successful businesswoman or an entrepreneur then it's merely equifinality. Those chose different paths to reach the same destination. My main concern is the representation factor placed upon black women wholly. Allow me to explain with this next segment.

On one occasion when I was invited to lecture an English class at Winston-Salem State University, Professor Michelle Leverett told me of the troubling story of Sarah Baartman (Saartjie Baartman), also called "Hottentot Venus." Sarah was a young South African woman who was said to have been born in 1789 and lived to be 26 years old before dying of an inflammatory ailment, possibly smallpox or pneumonia, in 1815. Sarah was a slave who had an abnormally large posterior (booty---to put it in modern terms.) Slave owners took full advantage of this abnormality and decided that they would profit off of this. Sarah was shipped off to Europe from South Africa and was made a public spectacle for white Englishmen. Historians say that Sarah was put in a cage naked and subsequently displayed for monetary profit. It has also been noted that Sarah herself partook of the profits from this exploitation. However, this has yet to be confirmed. Visitors were allowed to view her and for an extra fee, were also allowed to "touch" her. Although Sarah was said to have been highly intelligent and spoke fluent Dutch; she was merely looked upon and admired for her "assets." Sound familiar?

Sarah also suffered from a condition called *"sinus pudoris"* in which some African women had enlarged vaginal labia. Scientists were so enthralled by her condition upon her death; her genitalia were dissected and cast in wax. Her skeleton, preserved genitals, and surprisingly her brain, were all placed on display in Paris until 1974.

Contemporaries ignorantly came to the conclusion that Sarah's oversized genitalia were physical proof of African women's "primitive sexual appetite." Sadly, it wasn't until the year 2002, over 200 years after her death, that her remains were returned to her homeland in South Africa. This historical reference has several dimensions within it, which I would like to dissect.

It is very evident that the exploitation of the black woman's body has long been prevalent in history. I have read accounts where during slave trades the women were seduced and sexually demeaned by slave traders. Our women were made spectacles of and raped while onboard slave ships during their tumultuous journey to America. Also in my studies, I read accounts of where former slave women themselves told horrific stories of how they were forced to work in the hot sun naked while on their menstrual cycle. Even then their "masters" took advantage of them. I guess we will never know the severity of what really went on during those times. However, just the thought and vision of that alone will make a young man consider his actions towards his sisters.

I think we can all agree that most lucrative business in the Hollywood and entertainment realm is the business of sex. It is seemingly intertwined in almost every aspect of the culture. We see it in the obvious venues such as pornography. We also see it more and more, even subliminally, in things such as television commercials, sitcoms, reality shows, etc. I say that because this is not a section in this chapter to try to rid Hollywood of this element and condemn it to Hell. It's there and it's obviously not going anywhere. I am trying to bring this home for us as a people.

Maya Angelou, Oprah Winfrey, Harriet Tubman, Maxine Waters, Gladys Knight, Nikki Giovanni, Nina Simone, Jocelyn Elders, India.Arie, Jill Scott, Angela Davis, Assata Shakur, Sojourner Truth, Rosa Parks, Coretta Scott King, Chaka Khan, Condoleeza Rice, Alicia Keys, Ledisi, Erykah Badu, Althea Gibson, Mahalia Jackson, Phyllis Wheatley, Alice Walker, Terri McMillan, Diana

Hate My Face

Ross, Michelle Obama, The Williams Sisters, Lauryn Hill, Queen Latifah, Angela Bassett, and many more all represent strong, positive black women to us. These are the women, past or present, that we expect to portray or have learned *did* portray a certain amount of dignity and class about them. They spoke or do presently speak to us through music, movies, politics, sports, philanthropy, the arts, etc. Sure some of them may have had public battles and all have had private battles, however, in the grand scheme of things we knew or know these women to represent us and represent black women in a strong virtuous manner.

I look at my beautiful mother, Gwendolyn, who is by far the epitome of a strong, intelligent, wise, caring, spiritual, and integrity filled black woman. I'm sure many of us can and will say this about our respective mothers, grandmothers, etc. Black women are the seed bearers of our race. They are the matriarchs of our communities. They are the pillars and nurturers of our people. They should be the close second to God in the hearts and bosoms of black men.

In my mind, they are undoubtedly the most beautiful creation by God.

Sadly, as in Sarah's case, they have been downgraded to a gyrating piece of meat for lustful eyes and put inside a 21st century cage to be looked upon as 3/5 of a human being (if that). The sad thing is it is a black man, in most cases, who allows and promotes this travesty of the representation of the beautiful black woman. This is not only limited to videos and physical aspect of the exploitation of sisters. One can also look at certain reality shows and talk shows and see how the black woman is even being portrayed as overly feisty, argumentative, void and class and self-respect, vulgar, uneducated, materialistic "gold-diggers" as well. Comedienne/actress Monique made a very powerful statement during the reunion show of VH1's reality show "Charm School." She said how it deeply bothered her concerning the amount of letters and e-mails she received that referenced how the beautiful young black women cast on the show were sadly misrepresenting black women as a whole. I, too, had these exact thoughts. I will admit that I watched the show as well. I didn't necessarily watch it to see the outcome, though it was intriguing, I watched it in hopes that the next episode would not be as bad as the previous one. I often wondered how much of it was actually scripted. Was it really about seeing young women empowered to be better, or was it simply to show the world how "our sisters" supposedly interact with each other on a daily basis? I began to think about how many shows there were that portrayed them in a positive, non-overly combative light. There are not many, if any, besides Girlfriends or Living Single, which is merely in syndication. Just as it is with black men, it seems that Hollywood is getting rich off of the antics of angry black women as well. This is proof that we continue to allow ourselves to be set back as a people for a dollar; with black women as the hot commodity. We have to stop giving society a reason to label us. Sure it's entertainment, but it *is* called a "reality show" right? So what is this really saying to America?

The Respect and Love Element (The Partnership)

The Bible says in the book of Genesis chapter 2:18, *"And the Lord God said, It is not good that man should be alone; I will make a help meet for him."*
The first portion scripture is relatively simple to understand. God looked at Adam and decided that it was not good for him to be alone. The second portion of it marks the development of what may be the first partnership mentioned in the Bible. "[I will make a help meet for him.]" To put it plainly, God knew that Adam would need some help in order to meet his destiny. Let's look at this. In verse 18 God decided that it was not good for Adam to be alone. Biblical scholars have told me that there could be years in between verses. From verses 19-20 Adam had the task of naming every living creature of the field and fowl (bird) of the air. I would assume that this did not happen in the matter of one day. The scripture goes on to say that God then had to, first, create the creatures and then bring them to Adam for him to name them. Here again, I will

assume that this took even more time to do. Interestingly, in the latter portion of verse 20, after Adam named all of the creatures that God brought to him, the Bible says, "[but for Adam there was not found a help meet for him]." Keep in mind that this is merely my interpretation of this passage of scripture. Could it have been that even after Adam named all of the creatures of the air and all of the creatures of field (quite possibly taking many, many years), it dawned on him that *he* still felt "empty" in a sense? Here he had done what the Lord God Himself commanded him to do. The Lord found a helper in His creation Adam; yet, Adam still desires *his* helper.

Side note: *This is my argument for those men who spend all their time at church and neglect their wives and families. If doing what God commanded did not totally complete Adam; what makes you the exception?*

Keep in mind that God is Omniscient (all knowing), so of course, He knew what Adam needed and desired before Adam did. If you look at the beginning of verse 18, before God verbally gave Adam the mandate, He already knew that his loneliness was not good. In verse 21, God causes a deep sleep to fall upon Adam, and He took one of Adam's ribs and made a woman. A lot of people (at least in my experiences) seem to overlook the fact that here in the Bible the first surgery seems to have been performed. The scripture states plainly, "[and He took one of his ribs, AND closed up the flesh instead thereof.]" The point I am trying to make with this illustration is that a woman is as much of a part of a man as himself. God specifically took one of Adam's ribs and made woman so Adam could have a helpmeet, or helpmate to use modern day terms. I think this is all the proof in the world to let us know that a man NEEDS a WOMAN to be spiritually complete. Therefore, anything a man does to a woman he is indirectly or spiritually doing to a part of him. If a man loves a woman then he inevitably loves a part of himself. On the flip side of that, if a man is disrespectful or hateful to a woman, he also hates a part of himself. Knowingly or unknowingly, he will suffer the consequences or reap the rewards inwardly, himself.

Once a young man is taught the importance and value of a woman, he will have a greater concept of his responsibility to the woman in general. Also, once a young man is taught the importance of respecting what was created as a result of him in the beginning will force him to cherish woman. To respect someone and to feel responsible for someone has to be grounded, first, in love. Granted, we all make mistakes. I have disrespected women in my past and will probably do so again. Of course, I will make a conscious effort not to do so, but sometimes you can disrespect someone or offend someone and not be aware of it. However, I have learned that once disrespect is brought to one's knowledge, ask for forgiveness and restitution. You do this because you realize the fact that God specifically created woman to be your helper, partner, and mate. This is the reason why I am so adamant about why we, as black men, should not be so passive about how our women are portrayed today. Moreover, we should NOT be doing it ourselves.

Keep It Pimpin'

The "pimp movement", as I refer to it, is causing our young black men to not feel the need to respect any black women outside the ones in his immediate family. I recall when I was volunteering as a counselor at an after-school program. I remember one day as I was making my rounds with the students, a young man about the age of 6 gave me a picture that he had drawn in school. I wish to this day that I had kept that picture. The picture was drawn in your typical 6-year-old's interpretation of art. It was a stick figure of what seemed to be a man adorned with a rather large necklace with the heading of "Pimp" (properly spelled as well) on the drawing. Of course, I commended the young man on his drawing and knew that he really did not understand what he was portraying in the portrait. He was merely artistically mimicking what he had been exposed to as a result of probably TV or music. He was very proud of his drawing, as was I. I was more so proud of the effort, however, and not necessarily what was being represented. The sad thing was that he identified with "pimp" enough, even at his young age, to be able to interpret it in a drawing. He was 6 years old. They learn by seeing, even when we are not aware. I pray that he has been since taught the meaning of this and has strayed from this type of innuendo, or that he has come into the knowledge himself.

"I wonder why we take from our women
Why we rape our women, do we hate our women?
I think it's time to kill for our women
Time to heal our women, be real to our women
And if we don't we'll have a race of babies
that will hate the ladies, that make the babies" -Tupac- Keep Ya Head Up.

I recently read an article that spoke on the misogyny in hip-hop. One sister basically said that is what not necessarily the name calling that bothered her. She stated what hurt more was the fact that it seems brothers simply did not love their sisters anymore. Can you blame her for thinking this?

I think back to how the musicians of old literally worshipped black women in their music. Donny Hathaway, Luther Vandross, Lenny Williams, and countless others sang with great passion and adoration as it related to the women in their music. I give major props and respect to current artists such as NeYo, Eric Robeson, Raheem Devaughn, Dwele, Kem, and many more that still choose to value and respect women in their music. They see a beauty in women that apparently some of their less mature counterparts do not see or choose not to see. Possibly, their vision is skewed by a dollar sign.

Our young men have to be taught the value and the worth of black women. Whenever I am in the presence of a young brother and a young sister, I stress the importance of him opening up the door for her. My two nieces have grown accustomed to that even when they are with me. I do this so they will have a standard set when they come to the years of dating. Its little things like these that will make our young men respect their sisters, and more importantly, themselves. There comes with these little acts a sense of pride for themselves and accountability to our women. It seems that the problem is that our women are not being seen as a "priority," but more so as an "option" or "something to do."

The Necessity of a Sister's Love and Support

I remember my friend Marsha and me going to a rummage sale and I happened to run across this sister with a T-shirt on that simply said, "I still love black men." I asked her could I hug her because that shirt really touched me. She obliged and I told her, "Thank you for still loving me."

However, that shirt also made me think, "Have our sister's patience grown thin with us?" For her to have to profess that on a shirt was almost as if she was saying that she was possibly one of the few left that still loved us. I don't think that it's the fact of our sisters not loving us anymore; I feel it borders more on their faith in us to be there for them and to love them for who they are.

Upon writing this section of this chapter, I decided against looking at statistics and reading articles from Essence magazine, and other periodicals. Instead, I had lengthy conversations with 3 single sisters whose opinion and insight I hold in high regard. The responses between all three sisters were almost eerily identical.

They all said that they do, and always will, love black men. However, at this point in their life they are very *disappointed* in a great majority of black men. Of course, this is not targeting all black men. Keep in mind that they said they still love us and feel as if we will come back "home" one day. However, right now they are losing faith in us. There a lot of black women who feel like we as black men are failing them terribly. One will probably assume that I talked to three bitter sisters. That is not the case. One of them was in a very fulfilling relationship. The other two were very self-sufficient sisters with degrees, their own homes, and cars.

The response that resounded in me most was the fact they feel as if brothers are not appreciating them and valuing them as black women anymore. Several key elements were brought up amongst the three. They ranged from: open disrespect, the "Becky" syndrome (black men and white women), the laziness factors in some black men, and black men not stepping up to the plate as fathers.

The one statement that bothered me the most, however, was "I simply feel like black men don't love us (black women) anymore." That hurt me deeply. In all of my love, respect, adoration, and care for the black woman, I still felt like that one statement was directed at me. Not that she was saying that directly to me. However, because of the fact that I am a black man, I felt like it subliminally referred to me as well.

When the women who raise us, give birth to our children, support us, take our hands in marriage, and submit themselves to us as the head of the home begin to make statements such as this, we have a serious problem.

It seems as though the reason why we have an onslaught of the "independent black woman" now is simply for the fact they feel they can no longer depend on us as black men to help them. Carefully grasp what I said. I did not say "give it" to them. I said to simply "help" them. It seems there has been a stigma placed upon black women which states that they are money-hungry "gold-diggers" and attitudinally challenged. Of course, this does relate to some black women, but definitely not all of them.

In my short 34 years of life here on God's green Earth, two things I have learned about women (not just black women) is that they want to feel (1) loved, and (2) protected by their man. Women want to feel "covered." Love makes up to the spiritual element, and protection makes up the physical element. In my relationship experiences or even just my experiences with any woman ranging from my relatives, friends, it gives me a great sense of accomplishment when I can be there for a sister. Whether it be something as minor as giving a female co-worker some change to get a snack out of the vending machine, or something as significant as holding a girlfriend while she cries upon hearing about the death of a grandparent. I, personally, have lost women in my life for the fact that they felt like I was not there for them when they needed me. It took me a very long time to understand this. However, after really looking at things from a woman's point of view, I now understand exactly what was and is meant.

My mother told me once that a man has to hear the things that a woman is *not* saying in order to hear her properly. This leads me to believe that many men do not take the time to understand a woman.

I am totally convinced that most black women want nothing more than a strong brother upholding them, surrounding them, loving them, encouraging them, affectionately holding them, protecting them, cherishing them, understanding them, and trusting in them. I honestly feel like a lot of black women who are with "Peter" as opposed to "Dajuan" is because they feel like they have no other choice, or their patience has simply worn out as it relates to the brethren.

My pastor made a very profound statement in a sermon he delivered. He said that a man would never reach his full potential without a wife. This is not to say that a man cannot be successful without a wife. We know this is not necessarily true. However, what he was saying was that a man will not reach his *full* potential without a wife. It is naturally instilled into a woman to want to serve her man. Please do not misinterpret what I saying. I do not mean serve a man hand and foot. When I say serve I mean it to say, "to serve as." A good woman will be a sidekick in any capacity to her man in pursuit of his dreams. If he starts a business she would serve as secretary, bookkeeper, receptionist, or co-partner. If he is writing a book she would help with the research, finding a publisher, a cover designer, or even something as simple as helping with a catchy title. A woman will GLADLY be the single person wait staff for a husband who has opened up his first small restaurant until he has enough revenue to hire someone else. This is what I mean by "serve" her husband. I know this to be true because I have seen this many times.

One of my closest friends, and mentor, Mike, and his wife Alicia are perfect examples of this illustration. Mike came up with idea of opening a smoothie shop on a whim. I distinctly remember him starting off with a regular commercial freezer, a few blenders, a couple of tubs of ice cream, some frozen fruit, juice, the proper utensils, the rental of a small space, a dream, and most importantly a fiancée, who believed in his dream. They have since gotten married and now Mike has a chain of smoothie shops along with other prosperous business ventures, while Alicia has written a bestselling book entitled, "Destined for Success." Even to this day, if business is overwhelming, Alicia will drop whatever she is doing and go to "serve" her husband in whatever capacity needed as it relates to the shop. This is not to downplay Mike in any way, but I believe that he would not have been as successful as he is presently without the help of his wife. Mike has won several business awards since and never fails to mention his wife as his number one supporter and partner.

My point is that we have to reverse the thought process that is invading our young black men's perception of women that is plaguing them. They have to understand that a woman is a necessity. A woman should be placed right under God in their lives. I have begun to train myself to say that I "need" a wife, as opposed to saying a merely "want" a wife. I may *want* something today and not have any use for it tomorrow. A need, however, holds much more value. For example, a young man without transportation can *want* a Mercedes, but ultimately he *needs* a car. A want, in most cases, generally denotes some sort of upgrade for something a person already has or something that particular person simply desires. Generally, needs derive from the absence of something that is imperative to sustaining an element of one's life or being. If a person is $50 short on a past due light bill that is due for disconnection, they don't *want* that money; they *need* it. However, if a person is $50 short on a pair of the new Jordan sneakers that just came out; they merely *want* it. It's not a threat to their overall wellbeing. That is the problem with a lot of young black men's view of black women. They *want* them but feel that there is a not a general *need* for them.

Proverbs 18:22 says, "Whoso(ever) findeth a wife findeth a good thing, and obtains the favor of the Lord." If we look at this scripture reference here we see two positives. Not only does a man who finds a wife find a good thing, he also obtains favor with the Lord. The reason why I put this in here is because we have to begin to start letting our young black men see their sisters as "wives" or helpmates as opposed to just someone they can have sex with. Of course, the majority of young black men in their preteen and teenage years are not thinking marriage at this point in their lives. Their hormones are wild and raging. We were once that way. However, it has to be embedded into their psyche at an early age that black women (or women period, whatever their preference) are a necessity to their success, not underneath them or behind them, but beside them. One may wonder how I, being a single man, can have the audacity to make these statements. Well, it's simple. I watch and observe. I thank God that I am learning these things now while I am yet single, as opposed to learning them after a divorce or two.

***Side note**- I have since gotten married to the woman of my dreams and am practicing these very truths successfully.*

Teaching Them to Respect Sisters

Our young black men have to be FORCED to respect their sisters. If we see a young black man disrespecting a young sister, we should respectfully address it *if* it is the right time and place. There have been times where I have seen this type of disrespect take place in public and I knew it was my duty to correct that young man and have him apologize to her. Of course this has to be done with a great deal of discretion. I, being only 5'6, 175 lbs., am not going to confront a 6'2, 250 lb. brother in public on the way he talks to his girl. It's just not smart. This generally works with younger kids in their teens.

It seems that our young men have made money, the streets, and materialism their new "woman." They will worship it, kill over it, and make it a priority over every other aspect of their life.

Our young black men are subliminally being taught that money should be their number one love, and not the love of God, the woman, and the family. I recently heard a line in a rap song that really bothered me. The young man says, *"If I wasn't married to the streets it would be you."* Is this what we want our young men listening to? What message is this sending?

If our young men only understood that once a man follows God's order of authority and love then everything else would beautifully fall in place. True love of a woman will inevitably develop into the love of a family. Once the love of the family has set in we would see a metamorphic change in the negative perception of the black family that has long plagued us. However, as long as our young men continually see our sisters as a booty without a face, or merely a vagina attached to a body and not viewed as a priority, then whatever she produces will not be viewed as a priority either.

Teenage pregnancy rates are skyrocketing because our young women are not respected. The rape of teenage girls is skyrocketing because women are sometimes viewed as objects or "a piece." If they are shown on a video as just a piece of meat to be devoured, then some of our young black men are going to carry out that perception into real life. For a man to rape a woman, he HAS to see them as a soulless creature. He forcibly takes what he feels like he deserves with absolutely no concern for the body or mind of the woman. You would not do that to someone that you have been taught from a young age to love and respect. Of course, there are different ways of looking at this. Some men are just evil. The Bible says that the devil is the prince of the air. There are indeed evil spirits that just reside in the hearts of some men. That is an entire differently demonic force that has to be dealt in another arena, which I will not get into.

Our sisters need for us to protect them and nurture them with love and support. Most women are, by nature, reciprocators. If we love and support them they will turn around and do the same for us. Moreover, they have a significantly more amount of patience than most men have, which means they will wait for us to "realize" these things. I often say that we are living in a time where young black men as a whole cannot afford to be reckless and haphazard anymore as it relates to our sisters. Black women are, by far, the most oppressed creature in America, and possibly, on Earth. Not only are they black (one strike), they are women (two strikes). They are even deemed inferior to their own counterparts who are black men. Black men have it hard enough. When it gets to a point where the black men become "slave-owner" to the black woman, who can they turn to for support and protection? Again, this is not referring to every black man and woman. I know of several brothers who honor and respect black women to the highest degree. The most embarrassing thing is when we allow other cultures, specifically White America, to see us degrade our women.

Many blacks got upset at Don Imus for his comments. Our inner "Al Sharpton" came out. Was Imus wrong for making such remarks? Of course. Should the media have put hip-hop on the firing squad too? Yes. A lot of people disagreed with me on this. Here is my stance on the issue. Don Imus was wrong with what he said. It's a fact. However, it seems that we turn a blind eye to what our own young entertainers are saying, as if it's okay because, "We can do that to each other because we are black."

Would that have made the rape of our women aboard slave ships okay as long as black men were doing it?

It was our moment. I anxiously waited for one of these guilty rappers to step up to the plate and say, "I, too, am guilty of this. I need to change my lyrics a little." I do not recall any one of them doing this. Let me clarify one thing. I do feel that as a result of rap music playing into the equation, the emphasis was taken off of Don Imus. This I did not agree with. He was the main focus. Here we see another case of the black man being the fall guy in a sense. However, when you are comparing seemingly an entire culture with the remarks of one white man it cannot be a "hush, hush" thing. Think about it. It took a white man uttering the phrase, "Those are some nappy headed hoes" to raise the consciousness of Black America, even if but for a moment. Yet, our children hear this type of innuendo everyday, with parents standing right there I may add, and sometimes nothing is said. I would imagine that if I walked up to a random sister on the street and called her a "bitch" to her face, or a nappy headed hoe I would walk away with a sore jaw, either inflicted by her, or her boyfriend/husband.

Frequently, when I go to universities and lecture on hip-hop, I will take the time to print out derogatory rap lyrics pertaining to women and read them aloud. This, of course, is done with no music, no specific cadence or anything. These lyrics are merely read from a sheet of paper to the class. Every time this is done, the young women are hurt, shocked, and devastated by what they are reading. It is the same songs they have listened to over and over, however, it is done without a beat to cover up the blasphemy. I tell them, "He read these lyrics back to himself and deemed them acceptable." I always see a look of disgust and somewhat hurt on the young ladies faces as if to say, "Is this how he thinks of me, of us?" Interestingly enough, females are the highest consumers of hip-hop music. Wouldn't it be a beautiful thing if every demeaning and degrading lyric about a female was, instead, an uplifting and positive one? It could be the same dope track and the same lyrical skill with just a different message. I think back to Queen Latifah's song "**U.N.I.T.Y.**" where she bellowed out the powerful words for her sisters to repeat and her brothers to heed, "Who you calling a bitch?!" She demanded respect! Our sisters have to demand respect just as she did.

We need each other. Black men and black women are partners in life together. Look at Martin and Coretta, Malcolm and Betty, Ozzie Davis (RIP) and Ruby Dee, Barack and Michelle, and countless others. They were and are a team. Will there be issues, arguments, disagreements, and sadly even divorces in some cases? Yes. However, while they were together they made a difference. I cannot recall any song from my parent's era where a brother referred to a black woman as a "bitch" or a "hoe." We are living in a critical hour where black men simply cannot afford to treat their counterparts as three-fifths of a human being anymore. Our young black men don't need to see reality shows where a celebrity can have a house full of women at his disposal to see if he can 'find love.' That's eerily similar to picking out a slave. You remember the scene from "The Color Purple" where "*Mista*" was picking out his wife? Think about it. Sure, the women may be doing it for exposure but does that make it acceptable? Our women should not have to fight for a brother's love; their love should be fought for. I choose to close this chapter out with a universal letter I wrote to all black women some years back.

"Dear Sister"

On behalf of all black men on the world I want to ask you for forgiveness. We find ourselves in a state where we will do anything for the love of currency. Among these things is the degradation of our most precious gift; you. You, who birthed us into this world and gave us life... You who will be our will be our wife and seed bearer. You, who have, along side us, endured the injustices of slavery and racism and was lynched and beaten for simply having our backs. You, who must now turn on the radio and hear us calling you garden tools and female canines while trying to convince you that these are merely modern day urban terms to be used as a means of expressing respect and adoration. Please forgive us. We, who exploit you in our videos, having you wear scantily clad attire to, supposedly, have the world to admire our most precious ass-ets.

I guess we have yet to understand that us calling each other pimps and players is subconsciously portraying to our sons that women are beneath us and nothing short of faceless objects used for sex and money.

There is a theory I read about called the "Theory of Anarcho-Feminism" which simply talks about the oppression of women. The theory basically says that the liberation of women requires the ending of all forms of expression, but most first start at the root of male oppression, which is a form of exploitation within itself. What this is saying is that when we oppress you through means of slander and exploitation, we are really doing it to ourselves. Simply put, because we are oppressed within ourselves we can only dispense unto you what we have in us. In essence, I guess I should be asking you to forgive us for not knowing our own worth.

This all started back on the trading blocks in slavery days when we had our genitals fondled to see if we could produce strong bucks for future cotton pickers and farmers. We were subconsciously taught that our worth lied in sexual prowess. As time progressed, even though knowledge was abounding, we had it etched into our psyche that the body was a means of worth instead of the mind. Strangely enough, we have taken this fallacy and applied it to our own counterparts, you. This has sadly lead to "To THE windooooooow… to the wall." However, this is not an excuse, We have historical books and new found knowledge readily available to us to break this cycle of ignorance, yet we continue to feed our minds and our son's minds with utter garbage. Forgive us. Please, however, in your songs, do not acknowledge the fact that you will kill for us if we died in the drug game. Think about it, you do not die wrongfully in something that has proven that, more than likely, death is inevitable. This makes us feel like you accept our frivolous lifestyles. Please...please stop saying that you will hold our kilos of crack for us, "pop the glock" for us in the struggle, and leave a "nigga's" brains in his lap for us, and so forth and so on. This gives us a warped feminine perception of masculine affirmation. We both know that nothing gives us masculine affirmation better than "shorty who got they nigga's" back.

If you carefully dissect that scenario, we aren't wearing blackface anymore and doing the "jig" in our videos either. We get you to do it for us by, "dropping it like it's hot", "shaking it like a saltshaker", and "shaking it fast." Nevertheless, some of us have yet to understand true knowledge of self. Understand that when you allow us to call you certain demeaning colloquialisms and then not correct us, we feel as if you are accepting what we say; thus we look at it as some modern day term of endearment. However, the fact remains, that when we get upset with you, or brag to our boys about how you let us "hit" on the first night...we use the exact same terms. Think about that.

In closing, please demand respect from us sister. Do not, by any means, continue to let us use you for our own selfish gain. Understand that many of us are weak, and if you too are weak then we produce weak offspring, and the weak inevitably die off. Deep down inside we really love you. However, it us to YOU to let us know what kind of love is acceptable.

With an apologetic spirit,

S.I.L.E.N.T.W.A.R.

The Spiritual Divide

The human spirit.

The vessel in which all things derive from is the *spirit*.

The morality of a man evolves from his *spirit*. Our bodies are mere housing units for our *spirit*.

In this chapter I will attempt to explore why a great deal of young black men seem to have lost touch with their spirit man. Perhaps they have never been taught the value of getting in touch with this pivotal side of them, thus only living a life trying to live out things that has contacted their soul.

As you have probably already figured out, this chapter will further expose my spiritual side.

The reason why the majority of my poems and songs have positive content is because I consider myself a spiritual person. When a person grows into the consciousness of their spiritual side they see life in a whole different perspective. It weeds out negativity from the root. They begin to understand the power of what they speak; be it positive or negative. I have recently begun to train myself to make a conscious effort to only speak positive things when possible. I understand that this cannot be accomplished 100% of the time. However, if I speak negatively I will attempt to override it with some sort of solution in the positive sense.

The Difference between the Spirit and the Soul

Many people are under the assumption that the spirit and the soul are one in the same. This is highly untrue and can cause internal confusion. The soul consists of the mind, emotions, and thoughts. The mind only has two functions; memory and imagination. When a person acquires knowledge it is instantaneously banked into the memory section of the mind. The same goes for when a person reminisces about something. Ideas, dreams, goals are all birthed from the imagination sector of the mind. The soul (mind) of a person cannot function properly if there are no external factors present. I tend to look at it like this in any given situation: the mind states the facts, the soul intensifies the feelings, and the spirit weighs the options (conscious). Many people stop at their soul realm. This is why the majority of society lives under the "do what feels good" umbrella.

The Connection between Spirituality and Reading

One of the biggest misconceptions concerning the term "spirituality" is that it involves going to a "church" setting. Of course, church is probably the place where many black men get in touch with their spiritual side; but it is not the only place. Many people, such as me were probably raised somewhat more in touch with their spiritual side. Both of my parents are ordained ministers so I knew from an early age the importance of being in touch with the spirit. Even though I was raised in church my entire life, I acquired a great deal of my spiritual side by reading. I have always been an avid reader, which I feel is a gift from God. At an early age, I vividly remember randomly picking up books from my mother's library and just reading them, even if I didn't really understand the content. Reading, to me, was just as much an extracurricular activity as playing football in the front yard with my friends. As a result of reading a lot, one will begin to experience the opening of the soul and spirit.

If I could name one thing that really exposed me to my spiritual side, apart from reading the Bible, it would have to be reading books on the trials of African American people, past and present. To be more specific, it would be reading about slavery and civil rights struggles. A sad but true saying states that if you want to hide something from a black man, simply put it in a book. I have never really understood why we as black men stray from reading. I have often thought that it may have something to do with our collective attention spans. We have always been a people that love to be entertained and to entertain. We are an energetic, creative, and gifted people. Thus, this leads me to believe that we learn more by sight, and experience. It seems as though not a great deal of priority has been put on reading as it relates to young black men. During my brief tenure as a teacher, I tried to encourage the young men in my class to read as much as possible. Reading heightens imagination and knowledge immensely for anyone. Imagine if we, as a people, were to take the time to emphasize the importance of reading to our young black men the same we emphasize sports, I truly believe that they would excel more spiritually and begin to see life differently.

Anybody that is close to me knows how much I love and look after my nephew Josiah. One of the greatest things I love about my nephew is that he absolutely enjoys reading. It touches my heart to see him reading when I go to my sister and brother-in- law's house, I will walk into his room and see him buried in a book, sometimes, almost to a point where he barely acknowledges my presence. As a result of my nephew's reading habit, I see the above average maturity level he is at even in his innocent years.

Once a person develops the habit of reading, very rarely will you find them not doing so when the opportunity presents itself. I truly believe that reading causes one to grow, inwardly, in some form or fashion. Whether it is positive or negative content, fiction or non-fiction, reading makes a person more aware and always hungry for "truth" or enlightenment. Personally, I never take anything I see or hear on the news or TV at face value unless it is a VERY trusted source. I immediately search for the facts. This applies to televangelists and politicians. There is no better knowledge than acquired knowledge from one's own personal research. I say in one of my rhymes, *"I lost my virginity to knowledge when I opened up a book, better yet when the book opened me up...knowledge of self, that's what's up."*

Recently me, one of my good friends and his son were conversing over dinner. Not long before that they had taken a tour of the childhood home of Dr. Martin Luther King. During their visit they learned how, in the King household, they were instructed to read a newspaper article and memorize a Bible verse on a consistent basis at early ages. Of course, in those days, they were not distracted by the video games and Internet that we have available today, but I am pretty sure that this is one of the key exercises that created one the world's most influential and positive leaders. Writer Ray Bradbury makes a very profound point. He says, "You don't have to burn books to destroy a culture; just get the people to stop reading them." Renowned poet Ralph Waldo Emerson says this, "If we encounter a man of rare intellect, we should ask him what book he reads." African American playwright and photographer Gordon Parks also makes a riveting statement concerning reading, he says, "Now looking back on what helped me most, I see the answer in one word -- reading. Without it I would have remained in darkness -- without a solid approach to photography, motion pictures, poetry, painting, or music."

Simply put...reading is the avenue to new things, new ideas, and a transformed mindset.

The Black Church and Responsibility

This particular section may upset "religious" people. I will explore areas of the black church that may be a tad taboo.

From as far back as I can remember, my Sunday mornings consisted of sitting on a pew (or behind a drum set for my case) in a black church. This is the case for many black folk. Many of our fondest memories, comedic moments, disappointments, life changing messages and memorable characters stem from the Sunday Morning experience. Comedian Ricky Smiley is a master of portraying these characters. We vividly remember Sunday school, the usher board, the choir, Vacation Bible School, Easter and Christmas plays, choir anniversaries, revivals, and many other activities that make up the black church.

I have heard church being referred to as a "hospital" for the spiritually and emotionally wounded.

Webster's dictionary defines a hospital as an institution for the reception, care, and treatment of the sick and injured. Traditional hospitals are built solely for the purpose of reaching out to those who are at not at ease (diseased). Thus if the church is a "hospital" for those who are at spiritual or emotional "dis-ease", then we are to be ready to accept these "patients" when they arrive. Moreover, those that are even more at "dis-ease" are cared for *first*. They are sent to the emergency room, special wards, and intensive care wings, and cared for by the most experienced and tenured doctors and nurses. As I stated earlier, the church is probably the most popular place that a young black man will explore his spirituality. If that were the case indeed, then why is it that it seems more and more young black men are seemingly straying from the church? Let's explore this dilemma.

I will venture to say that the young black men who struggle with the lack of the love the most do not understand why they are that way. They may not be cognizant of the fact that they are even like that. When a person first becomes diseased (in some cases) there are little to no warning signs. This is why we get routine check-ups and physicals from the family doctor. We, as a church going Christian community, will play the role of the "family doctor" in this scenario. It takes an exercise as simple as flipping the remote control to the local and national news to see the warning signs of the epidemic of a loveless generation of young black men that is upon us. We see the onslaught of black on black murders, kids barely in their teens getting felony charges and the rape of their own sisters. Yet, instead of rushing to their aid while warning signs have not yet developed into a full-blown disease, we sit, watch, and judge. When a doctor sees a patient on a routine visit, he or she usually asks the patient about their lifestyle. They inquire about their eating habits, whether or not they have an exercise regimen, and other activities they may be involved in. This is simply called, "getting to know or assessing the patient."

After this evaluation the doctor will give the patient a synopsis about what needs to be changed and what needs to stay the same. He doesn't judge them, tell them how bad a person they are, or belittle them because of their lifestyle. After all, the patient did come there for "help." The doctor's only purpose is to help the individual live an overall more fulfilled and healthy life.

Please keep in mind that the observations I am about to expound on do not reflect all black churches. However, if some things I say upset you then you may very well be dealing with a guilty conscience.

I have yet to visit a hospital that turns away patients simply because they do not dress like doctors and nurses. The workers at the hospital understand that the patients are not going to look like them, have the wealth of knowledge that they have achieved, understand the majority of the medical terminology in which they speak, or be 100% willing to accept their treatment options or advice. The church should be mimicking this, but do we? I will get back to this in a second. Let me, first, digress.

In the book of John chapter 21, verses 15-17, Jesus and his disciple Peter are having a very interesting dialogue. To paraphrase, Jesus is basically asking Peter repeatedly, "Do you love me?" Of course, Peter is answering the question by saying, "Lord, you know I love you." If you take the time to read these few verses it's almost as if it was (to use a modern term) "cut and pasted" scripture. Every time that Peter proclaimed his love for Jesus; Jesus simply replied, *"Feed my sheep."* However, a point that must be made is that in the first scripture Jesus specifically said, *"Feed my lambs."*

Let's look at this for a minute.

Hate My Face

Most people would assume that a sheep and a lamb are the same creature. In actuality they are, however, a lamb is a *young* sheep. A lamb is also defined as a gentle or innocent person, and one who is easily misled. I don't think it is merely coincidental that Jesus specifically mentioned the "younger generation" of sheep **first**. In Verse 18, Jesus clarifies why He separated the two in the scripture. He says this (Amplified version): *"The truth is, when you were young, you were able to do as you liked and go wherever you wanted to. But when you are old (older), you will stretch out your hands, and others will direct you and take you where you don't want to go."* If the term "feed" in this passage of scripture means to care for, lead, nurture, teach, and impart substance into, I am almost certain that Jesus was basically saying, "Reach out to them while they are young (lambs) so they will not become [*sheep* who have been led astray.]" (Isaiah 53:6).

It is pretty evident that Jesus' main purpose was and is to reach out to those who are lost. If we (church folk) are followers of Christ, then we should be mimicking the actions of Jesus.

My question, thus, is whether or not we are doing that?

One of the best things I love about my church is it's passion for outreach. Our edifice is merely the building we worship in, but our actual "church" really begins when we go outside of the four walls.

It seems to me that great deals of our young black are not drawn to church simply because they do not feel welcomed there. Walking into a church for them is no different from walking into a bank or a store. They are stared at because they "look different," dress different, or possibly even look threatening in a sense. The only difference is that more than likely they are going to have to walk into a store or a bank eventually. One needs money, food, clothing, etc. However, there is really no need (in their mind) to walk into a church, especially if you are being looked at suspect *even* in there. Some churches seem to become more of a social club than a "hospital." It's almost as if you have to look a certain way, dress in the latest fashion, or get some sort of membership or induction. Sad to say, but it's almost as if we have strayed away from Jesus' original mission and constructed our own agenda. The church is supposed to exemplify love, compassion, understanding, and a giving spirit. These are the elements that our young black men are yearning for. If we are supposedly portraying that, then why are they walking away from church? Think about that.

The Element of Confusion in the Black Church

One surefire way to cause a person to get out or not be involved with something or someone is to simply confuse them. Confusion causes frustration and frustration often leads to giving up or quitting. If a person sees something that may confuse them from the gate, they probably will not involve themselves with it. Church is supposed to be a place where people see other people who reflect the image and likeness of Christ. Of course, I am not saying that the church is a place full of perfect people. However, what I am saying is that the church should not be a place where a young black man leaves more confused than he was when he entered through the doors. The church is supposed to be set apart from the "world." It should be a place where someone can come and feel at ease, but at the same time feel challenged to become a better person, and a more spiritual and righteous (not self-righteous) individual.

I have to call things like I see them, and, to be honest, in some cases the black church seems to have become a circus of utter blasphemy against God's original purpose for its existence.

I can say this because I have never left church and have bore witness to the fact that it has gotten progressively worse. I can pretty much say the church, itself, has become its own patient.

The true spiritual aspect of the black church seems to almost have faded into oblivion.

If a young black man can go into a church and see the exact same elements he sees in a world that he wants to pull away from, what good is the church offering him? As I stated before there is no such thing as a perfect church, but when that young man looks into the stained glass windows and sees mostly stained "saints" he will be confused. It is the equivalent of someone going into the hospital and seeing other sick people acting as if they are healed of their ailment, and looking at the person as if *they* are "afflicted."

Many churches in modern times are into the trend of "reaching out to the youth." I think that this is a great idea, and also there are many, many churches that are doing this with a great deal of class and effectiveness. God has blessed me to be able to speak at many youth conferences and "minister" through the gift of spoken word. I have witnessed many lives changed through the words that God has given me to speak. I did not have to look like "so and so" rapper to accomplish this. Granted, I did speak in a dialect that the children understood and could relate to. I have seen even the hardest of young men shed tears after I spoke candidly about the life that God wants them to have, the love that God has for them and the immeasurable grace and forgiveness that God gives to them. There were some places I have spoken at, however, that I left confused and even somewhat hurt in a sense. I will explain.

The generation of children that we are facing now has to have radical solutions to deal with radical problems. When I grew up we didn't have the pressures that kids are dealing with now. It wasn't all about money, sex, jewelry, how hard you were, and drugs. Rarely, if ever, did you hear about school shootings, gangs in school, gay and lesbian clubs in high school, drugs, teacher and students involved in sexual relationships, and many more issues. My point is that the methods they used in church in the 1980's and '90s are simply not going to work in this generation. This means that we definitely need somewhat extreme approaches in order to reach today's youth. I have to say this because I do not want anybody to think I feel like that memorizing Amazing Grace is going to be very effective in reaching our youth.

I understand that we (adults) have to realize that kids are going to be kids regardless. Besides, we were once kids as well. In all of our hardheadedness, child-like knowledge, stubbornness, selfishness, and "untamedness", we (to all those who this applies to) were eventually reached and became civilized adults.

There has to be a line between merely relating to children and actually reaching them. In some events I have been at, it stopped at relating to them.

I distinctly remember a "youth jam" I was invited to speak at that nearly made me not want to speak at another church youth event. I am sure this particular church had good intentions but the things I saw take place, I'm sure, were not just noticed by me. There was a particular portion in the service where the kids were allowed to "get their praise on." I honestly believe that somewhere in the kid's minds they heard "get your freak on." With the children's parents standing right there essentially rooting them on, I had to remember that I was in a church and not a club. As I sat there with my mouth literally agape, I watched these children freak and grind on each other like they were auditioning for a 2 Live Crew video. It was interesting to say the least. These children were dropping it like it was hot, booty shaking, "pop, lock and dropping it", and "getting low" with the best of them. As I waited for at least one adult to come and minimize the "freakage", I instead heard, "Go ahead and praise Him." I understand that God doesn't change, but His methods do. This, however, could not have been pleasing in His sight. I am not blaming the children at all. Essentially, they are going to do what they are allowed to do. I blame the adults for not stopping this when they saw it getting out of control. As the "praising" begin to wind down the next thing that happened really bothered me. Within literally five seconds the children shifted from "getting crunk" to "holy dancing" or "shouting"(as we like to call it) upon command of the pastor. They immediately went from "getting low" to "lifting up holy hands" and running around the church in "spirit-filled" celebration almost instantaneously. Could this be sending the wrong message to our children? It seemed as if this exercise was subliminally saying to our kids that "getting spiritual" is some sort of internal switch that can be turned on and off at will, whenever it is deemed necessary.

Amidst of all of this I chose to remain optimistic the best I could. After this ceased, the pastor proceeded to give an altar call (an invitation to accept Christ). In my mind, it seemed only "spiritually" fair that the same amount of time that the children were given to freely express themselves in dance should be the same amount of time given to them to consider accepting Christ into their life. This was not the case.

The invitation may have lasted two minutes at most. Inevitably, none of the children accepted the call. Sadly, not only did they not accept the call, but also within minutes "the party" began again and the dance floor was once again a free-for-all.

My point is this. The event *related* to the children, but did it really *reach* them? This leads to one aspect of confusion. A child does not need to come to church events such as this and see and do the same things that he or she sees in the secular world. This will lead him to think there either there is no need for church, or that he can proclaim "spirituality" yet have no evidence of a spirit led life. There has to be some dividing line that exhibits a changed lifestyle. A hospital that employs nurses and doctors with the same ailments and failing health as their patients will not be a very effective hospital. The same goes for the church. The church should not look EXACTLY like the secular world. Am I saying that all men should wear bishop collars and the women should all wear ankle length dresses? No. What I am saying is that in our attempts to reach young black men, no matter the extremity, we should focus more on being effective as opposed to being more "hip" in our approach.

Men Worshipping God through Their Character

While I am on the subject of the spirituality I have to mention the need for young black men to see real men earnestly worshipping God through their *character*. Often times I think we as church folk view worshipping God as merely lifting our hands in church, or praising God with song or a dance. Although this is a form of worship; worshipping God is a lifestyle. Worship is merely a way of displaying allegiance to God. Thus we worship God through everyday living. Going to work to provide for your family is worshipping God. Displaying Godly character in the midst of temptation is worshipping God. Treating your wife with respect and love is worshipping God. Providing a Godly example for a young man to follow is worshipping God. Anything that exemplifies the will of God is worship.

Character is commonly defined as the complex of mental and ethical traits marking and often individualizing a person, group, or nation. I have heard character defined more in depth as, "who you are when no one is looking."

I will choose to look at character on a broader scale for the sake of my point.

One of the truest statements is that a young man will do what he sees an older man do before he does what the older man *tells* him to do. Young men will mimic what they see people in "authority" over them do. We all did. I do things that my father did to this day, and sometimes I do not realize it until later on. My mother tells me that I am getting more and more like my father (stepfather) with certain things I do and how I handle certain situations. I picked up these traits because of things I saw, and not necessarily things I heard him say. A person can say certain things, and then do the exact opposite of whatever they are professing. The thing a person actually *does* is a true testament to character. This is portrayed a lot with people in positions of power. Politicians who claim to be moral and just men and women often get caught up in scandals involving adultery, and financial corruption. This is, sadly, also true with men of the cloth. It saddens me that so many pastors and evangelists are caught up in sexual scandals, both heterosexual and homosexual.

I understand that all sin and fall short of God's glory. No one is immune to falling prey to temptation. You fall down and you get up. It happens. It's life. However, I feel like that has to be a conscious effort made on the part of adult black men to portray Godly character, or even simple moral character in front our younger generation. Often times I see men complain about how bad and mischievous their sons are, yet never realizing their sons are only mimicking them. If you constantly cuss in front of your son, more than likely they will cuss as well. If you disrespect women in front of your son, more than likely they will disrespect women as well. A tiger cannot train his cubs to be a lion. They will do what see portrayed in front of them.

One issue that I see in some older black men is that they have the wrong idea of what true manhood is. I think manhood is misconstrued as simply holding down a job, paying your bills, taking care of your family, and/or being involved with a woman. Don't get me wrong, these are all great things, but they do not necessarily portray *true* manhood in its totality. Often times it seems that manhood is portrayed by how tough a man is physically. However, being a spiritually tough man is greater. It is a fact that all men struggle with some character flaws. I have many. I work on them daily. At times, I fall victim to them. Other times, I overcome them. It's an ongoing battle.

Older men who have young men looking up to them have to be really careful about how they carry themselves. One thing my pastor always says is that, "Someone is always eating from your tree." Black men have to be more accountable for their actions portrayed in front of the younger generation. By the grace of God, I have a lot of young men who look to me for guidance and direction. I also have friends my age, and older, who look to me for spiritual advice and prayer. With this being said, I can't do certain things I did 5 or 10 years ago. My nephews and I joke and play around a lot, however, they know that sometimes I have to really be an "uncle" to them, and tell them life lessons they need to hear. I have to correct them if they are wrong or out of line if they're fathers are not around. They know when they can call me "unc," and when to use "yes sir," and "no sir." It is imperative that our young black men know that they have to respect us, all while being comfortable enough to able to come to us for advice or help. It seems as if it has come to a place where we as older black men are too busy still trying to fit in with the younger crowd, thus leading to them to think that they don't have to mentally mature. I get tired of seeing 45 year old brothers still sagging their jeans. Don't get me wrong, it's okay to be young at heart. I am. However, I realize that

I have to dress, think, and act as a grown man. All of this incorporates character. The Apostle Paul says in 1Corinthians 13:11, "When I was a child, I spake as a child, I understood as a child, I thought as a child: but when I became a *man*, I put away childish things." Older black men need to learn to relinquish those childish things. These things could be childish thoughts, childish words, childish ways, and childish reactions to situations. We have to learn how to portray character. I thank God that I was fortunate enough to have men in my life that showed good character around me. Sadly, many of our young black men do not have that blessing.

Black Men and Sexuality

In the chapter entitled, "Cherishing Our Treasures" I speak on the issue of black sexuality quite a bit. I did not, however, speak specifically on the black male sexuality viewpoint. In case you are wondering why I chose to put this topic in the chapter about spirituality, it's because spirituality and sexuality are closely related. To use as an example, in Marvin Gaye's song entitled "Let's Get It On", Marvin says in one verse, "If the spirit moves you, let me groove ya." Then he goes on to say, "I've been sanctified." To be sanctified means to be holy, purified, sacred, or consecrated. Interestingly enough, Marvin sings this is in a song about sexual intercourse. That act of having sex makes him feel pure, holy even. Perhaps, Marvin was saying that he had now been sanctified, or purified enough to have the honor of lying with this specific person who he was singing about. In any case, the point I am making is that sexuality and spirituality plays a major role in the lives of black men. Sexuality is a beautiful thing if done in the correct context. God wants sexual relationships to be beautiful, creative, and on a regular basis between a husband and wife. The Song of Solomon is full of sexual innuendo as Solomon poeticizes his lover. This is proof that God has created us to enjoy sexual relations. Sex, however, has become a perverted act for many black men and society in general. It seems to have been downgraded to some sort of panty counting contest. As I stated earlier, I cannot say that I remained a virgin until marriage. I can honestly say now that married sex and premarital sex are totally different. It's a spiritual element that is attached to married sex that one does not get from pre-marital sex. For the most part, the majority of people are not going to wait until marriage before they experience sexual intercourse, thus, I am not going to go on a tirade about abstaining from sex before marriage. I couldn't do it. Though I can't deny that I wish I would have waited, and that it is the right thing to do, the truth is, most people are not going to do it. Let's just be real.

There is a stigma attached to black men concerning sexuality. Most notably, that we are sexual deviants who, according to myth, are well endowed "Mandingos" who love as much sex as we can get, all while ignoring the consequences. Even during my years of fornication, I never lost my earthly morals. Not saying this was an excuse.

However, I am grateful to this day that I was always "safe." The reason why I brought this up is because it bothers me the amount of black men that still engage in unsafe sex practices. With the amount of diseases and unwanted pregnancies, it bothers me that this doesn't deter more men from having unprotected sex. It's the equivalent of planting a seed, and then praying for crop failure. I believe that this is far more than seeking the enjoyment of pleasure, and hoping nothing happens. I think it is a spiritual thing.

I recall some years back watching a television talk show where the guests were men with a high number of sexual partners. Specifically, there was a brother on there who claimed to have had unprotected sex with more than 900 women. When asked did he worry about catching STDs, he said, "I'm immune to diseases." He didn't say it jokingly either, he was serious. I begin to think about how many black men may actually have this same mindset. It bothers me the amount of black men that are literally spilling their seed in every garden they can without being responsible. "Heterosexual" men who have unprotected sex with other "heterosexual" men (still haven't figured this one out) are bringing HIV home to their women at alarming rates. For a person to sleep with someone they claim to love knowing they are infected with a disease with absolutely no cure, and not wear protection is not something a man operating under a stable mind state can do. That is spiritual wickedness. It goes beyond flesh, and blood. Pure evil is what it is. I say in one of my songs, *"Uncouth, indiscreet down low brothers plus no rubbers equals mother's burying their daughters....something's in the water."* I tried very hard to evade the issue of black men and homosexuality in this book, but I have to touch on it. HIV is among the highest killers of black women in this country. Why? Love. Our women are looking for love and will overlook many things to stay with a man that she knows is whorish. Notice that I didn't say men that are "dogs." A "dog" is merely a man who sleeps with other women besides his significant other. A whore will sleep with anything for some sort of satisfaction. A prostitute engages in sex for financial satisfaction. A whore sleeps with anyone in attempts to feed a sexual satisfaction that can never be fulfilled. The flesh is the complete opposite of the spirit. They cannot be in control of human at the same time. In every situation we are either obeying our flesh or our spirit. The spirit seeks love. The flesh seeks satisfaction.

I will get back to this later on in this chapter. First, allow me to explain how the media advertises to black people through soft whispers.

Subliminal messages are sometimes very loud. The other day I was watching TV with my wife and asked her when she last saw a Mickey D's commercial *without* a black person. She couldn't answer. Then I immediately saw that light bulb in her head come on. It's subliminal advertising catering to black people in order to keep us unhealthy. Specifically speaking about mainstream media, think about this. When was the last time you saw a black man in a condom commercial? How often do you see a black woman in a birth control pill commercial? How many times have you witnessed a commercial for a positive dating website, where they boast of making marriages happen, and seen an all-black couple? Here again, it's subliminal (non)advertising to blacks. Granted, there are these types of commercials, however, are shown on "all black" channels, late at night, and are referred to as a "hookup" line. The silent message that is being sent is that they want us to believe that we do not need to use condoms, and they are not interested in us (black folk) wanting relationships that lead to committed marriages. On the flip side, however, they will put big dollars into "special" jean advertisements, or other elements of the sort that glorify the proportions of the black female posterior, knowing that this will heighten our sexual craving. With us being creatures of sight, we in turn, go after these women. Our lust is heightened, we spot our prey, and like animals, we attack. I could name many songs that speak on the sexuality of black men. These songs are heavily played on our radio stations, and videos. The market is catered heavily to promoting the undisciplined sexual lifestyles of black men. Several movies are based on the sexuality of the black male. These different images and themes are etched directly into our psyche and played out through our reality.

In the book of Judges, the Bible tells the story of Samson; most notably, the story of his relationship with Delilah. If you carefully read this story you will see that Samson and Delilah played each other, in a sense, with Samson receiving the bad end of the deal. Keep in mind that Samson yearned for Delilah after he had already been with a prostitute beforehand. I mention this because it shows that Samson was a sexually charged individual. I think it would have been left out of the Bible had if it held no weight within the context of the story. Samson, like black men, was a powerful man, and a beautiful woman was "advertised" to him to find out his weakness. Obviously (to use a modern term), Samson was digging Delilah. Meanwhile, after the lords of the Philistine people got wind that Samson was in town, and found out he was checking out Delilah, they committed to finding out his strength by having her use her sexuality against him. Delilah was obviously sexually involved with Samson on numerous occasions. Each time she asked him to give the secret to his strength to her, he "played" her. He kept lying to her with different methods as to how he could be stripped of his strength. Finally, after several attempts, Delilah must have done something different to Samson in order for him to disclose his secret. Samson eventually told her that his strength was in his hair. Keep in mind that the scripture says that Samson told her, "When he knew he loved her." Delilah cut his hair, Samson was captured, had his eyes plucked out, and eventually died mainly because of his lust.

The reason I mentioned this story is because it parallels the way black men are sexually conned in today's society. Black men are strong men. Society marvels at our strength and seeks to find out how to drain us of this very element. They wonder how we continue to survive in the midst of an unfair world. How did we overcome slavery, civil rights, and injustice, and end up in The White House? They know the prowess, ingenuity, and intelligence of black men and seek to drain us of that strength. How do they do it? One of the ways is through sexuality. Our "Delilahs" come in all shapes, forms, and sizes. They cater to our lust through images on TV, magazines, and videos. Our "hair" is our love. Not our physical hair, but our strength. Society, after years and years of finding out where our strength lied, got the shears and cut off our love supply. They train us to demean ourselves subconsciously by boasting of how many women we have slept with, or how many baby mommas we have. This is a slow death for black men. As in Samson's case, many of us do not realize until it is too late, and we die off. The down low syndrome, HIV infections, unwanted pregnancies that lead to abortions, all attribute to the unknowing genocide of our people. They are the equivalent to us, as black men, trying to search for our identity with eyes that have been cut out, as we are wondering aimlessly looking for another "piece" to try and define our masculinity. The root of all these things is a warped perception of love downgraded to lust. We are dying, as a people, because of undisciplined and unrestrained sexuality. Unfortunately, Samson's only way out of his bondage was through death. Hopefully, if black men will grasp hold to the true meaning of love, they will not have to take this route.

We have to learn that sex and love are two totally different things. A good friend of mine, Sean, wrote a powerful piece called "Love." In it he says a very powerful thing. He says that it's funny how when two people have had sex, they were considered to have "made love", when that is far from the truth. If we, as black men, will learn that sex is a powerful force that means more than achieving an orgasm, we can grow. I never knew what real lovemaking was until I made love to my wife for the first time on our honeymoon night. I truly learned the value of love.

Being Careful With Religious Experimentation

Hate My Face

Staying in the vein of religion I have to mention this. There are several religions out here that our young black men can choose from. In my travels of performing and lecturing, I have been blessed to come across many gifted young brothers. I truly believe that God puts certain people in your life for a reason. I remember a few years back I had a chance to lecture at Carver High School in my hometown of Winston Salem. I was invited by my high school journalism teacher, Dr. Felicia McMillan. There was a young man who got up in front of his class and recited a freestyle piece (a poem that is not written) that literally blew me away. His name was Marco. I instantly felt a spiritual connection with this young man and we have kept in contact since. He calls me "pop", and I call him "son." Marco is, by far, the most gifted young poet I know. His ability to express himself through poetry is phenomenal and soul stirring. Marco and I talk a lot. We often talk about the black experience and religion. It was at one point, however, that I noticed Marco had become very impressionable as it related to different religions. It seems as though every time we talked he was experimenting with some new belief. I have never been one to drive my Christian beliefs down another person's throat. I truly believe that your Light shines the brightest when you do not know someone is looking. When you can exude the love of Christ unknowingly, people take heed and inquire. One thing I always told Marco was to be careful what you allowed into your spirit. I never, however, swayed him from studying and seeing what was real and what was not. I believe that you can learn something from any religion, besides religions that totally defy God. I think Islam had some very valid and effective teachings and nuggets as it relates to black men. I believe that the Nations of Gods and the Earths (5 Percenters) teachings of Knowledge of Self are very impactful to a certain degree. My issue comes only when certain religion's teachings begin to teach there is no need for a "god."

I think once we begin to worship trees and pray to the wind, we have gotten off base. I believe that Jesus is God's son and that He died on the cross for my salvation. That is my belief and I choose to live by that. The teachings of the Bible guide me in my everyday endeavors. There is nothing in the Bible, as you can see in this book, which cannot relate to present day life if dissected correctly. The whole premise of the Bible is love. I feel that any religion that makes love secondary, and law primary is simply not a good religion. I also feel like any religion that is simply a text of laws and exhibits no form of ministry to a person's spirit is simply a waste of time and energy. I am not some religion expert so there is really not much for me to expound on when it comes to this subject. However, I said that to say our young black men need their soul and spirit's touched, and I feel like Christianity does this effectively when done with a pure heart.

Our Responsibility to Impart Spirituality

We have to understand that the very issues we sweep under the rug are the same issues that will permit us to see more and more our young black men being taken under. It is evident that society has an agenda specifically designed to bind the hands, hearts, and minds of young black men. It is OUR responsibility to bring these things to light and DEAL WITH THEM. We can protest, picket, march, and rally all day until we can no longer walk; but if we don't bring it (the conspiracy) to the attention of the targets (young black men) first, then we are fighting a useless battle. We have to be honest with our young men. This must start at home. We cannot rely on the TV, radio, the schools, and even the church to develop spirituality in our young men. At some point or another all of these elements have failed them. I am not saying that they haven't done some good because, in some form or fashion, they have. I have had many teachers, coaches, celebrities, pastors, and others to play a part in me recognizing the importance of the spiritual side. However, in the grand scheme of things, it began from what I saw in the home.

Did I grow up in a picturesque home full of love and perfection? No. Did I see my parents argue and fight? Yes. Did I make mistakes? Plenty. However, I was taught spirituality by the mistakes I made and the mistakes I saw my parents make, then seeing the lessons in them and being taught from a realist point of view.

Perhaps the greatest exhibit of spirituality is to see someone (or family) make a 180-degree turn from the person or people they *used* to be. It will make a young black man realize that there is indeed, a force greater than what is seen to the natural eye. They are not going to learn the importance of spirituality by watching music videos that smother them with materialism. This type of exhibition only strokes their flesh and nothing more. Granted, it heightens the imagination and will cause them to want to succeed in life, but you have to consider the source it derived from.

Black people have always been a spiritual people. A lot of our music *used to* exemplify this. It's amazing to me that "black" music has always had the attachment of either the spirit or soul with it. In the early days, primarily during periods of slavery, what we call hymns nowadays were called "Negro Spirituals." I would imagine that they were called spirituals because considering the pain, depression, injustice and agony they were experiencing, they still had enough determination, and love in them to sing songs to God. Strength had to come only from one's spirit. As time progressed and blacks began to see a difference and a "changing of the guard" in a sense, songs became more upbeat, energetic, joyous, promising, and filled with a sense of deliverance from oppression. Music for us had thus transformed from "Negro Spirituals" to "soul" music -not "Negro" soul music- but soul music. I will venture to say that it was called "soul" music because everybody could enjoy it. It had a "racially personalized" meaning for us, but could be enjoyed universally, by everyone. It's this element of black folk that we seem to be straying further and further away from. I have long said that it seems as if black people are losing touch with their spiritual side as a whole, not just the young men.

My favorite author and poet, Howard Thurman, says these words in his book, <u>The Inward Journey</u>.

"The miracles in the spirit? What are they? The resolving of inner conflict upon which all the lances of the mind have splintered and fallen helplessly from the hand; the daring of the spirit that puts to root the evil deed and the decadent unfaith; the experiencing of new purposes which give courage to the weak, hope to the despairing, life to those burdened by sin and failure; the quality of reverence that glows within the mind, illuminating it with incentive to bring under the control of the Spirit all the boundless fruits of knowledge; the necessity for inner and outer peace as the meaning of all men's striving; the discovery that the Covenant of Brotherhood is the witness of the work of the Spirit of God in the life of man and the hymn of praise to Him as Thanksgiving and Glory!"

The Bible declares that the fruits of the spirit are thus: love, joy, peace, long-suffering, kindness, goodness, faith, mildness, and self-control. The scripture then goes on to say (Galatians 5:22-23), that "against such things there is no law." To put this in its most simple terms, when these spiritual elements are exhibited there are no spiritual laws broken. God sees that person as a model "spiritual citizen."

In Mark 8:36, the Bible makes a much quoted statement, "What does it profit a man to gain the whole world and lose his soul?" Many Christians use this scripture in reference to a person dying without coming into the knowledge and/or accepting of the salvation of Jesus Christ. I, too, agree with this reference. However, I also tend to look at this as in reference to a person who is alive and well. Perhaps it was also referencing a person who seems to have it all as far as materialistic wholeness is concerned. This person has the Bentleys, the ice, the women, the money, and yet never grasps the beauty of living life on a spiritual plateau. Of course one can have material treasures and be spiritual simultaneously. However, if you look closely at the scripture and dissect; it paints another picture. The scripture says, "What does it profit a man to gain the *whole* world?" This can be meant to say that a man could gain the "wholeness" of the world. In other words, by the world's standards this particular individual could be living in what is perceived as completeness. Thus, this goes beyond simple material wealth. This also could include education, a family, and other intangible things. Then the scripture concludes by saying, "and lose his soul." One of the uses of the word "and" is as a conjunction, ie., "as well as." So this can also mean that this person can have possession of the whole world *and* also be losing his soul at the exact same time. This is simply another way of looking at this scripture. A person can lose his soul while living if non-spiritual things even things that are not deemed "bad" overcome him. The point that I am trying to make is that living a life without a spiritual connection/guide/backing will result in an unfulfilling life. We all need to rely on spirituality to be overall better humans. This includes treating each with respect, loving one another, agreeing to disagree, and being compassionate towards other folk shortcomings.

If our young brothers were to grasp this concept we would see a metamorphosis in them. Our beautiful young brothers seem to be lacking this type of teaching and guidance. So much emphasis is put on how hardcore they are, how little they cry, who gets feared the most, how big their money stack is, how many times they've been locked up, or how many women they have slept with, etc. Hardly anyone is taking the time to reach their spirit.

Perhaps a great deal of our young men is dealing with a "wounded masculinity." Many men may have been molested as children. Some young black men may feel as though spirituality is more of a "feminine" act. Any degree of spirituality is probably going to consist of a man submitting himself to a "higher power." When this comes about, perhaps the young man is dealing with the deception of a "lessened masculinity" in a sense. I have read that when a man is suffering from a "wounded masculinity" then the solution must be spiritual. We have to begin to impart spirituality within our young black men early in life. This can consist of having them to say prayers at night, reading something enlightening on a regular basis, spending quality father-son (or father figure-son) time with them, or simply talking to them (showing concern).

I distinctly remember when I was a counselor at a group home for behaviorally and emotionally challenged young men. There was a particular young man who was the "terror" of the house. One night while the other children were trying to sleep he was on a literal rampage. He was throwing things, trying to pick fights with the other boys, cursing, etc. After hours of trying to calm this young man down something inside of me said, "He just needs some attention." I finally got him in a room with just him and myself. I put my arm around him and simply hugged him. He instantly calmed down. I looked at him and said,

"That's all you wanted wasn't it?" His teary reply was, "Yes sir." His premature masculinity would not allow him to outwardly say that. It had to be identified spiritually. That hug was a spiritual act. I didn't have to read him 300 scriptures or perform an exorcism. It was a simple solution. Often times we make things too hard as it relates to spirituality. Instead of talking *at* our young men, perhaps we should try talking *to* them. Phyllis Martin, a former co-worker of mine during my tenure as a teacher had this saying in her classroom, "There are 3 (*A*)s every child needs: acceptance, attention ,and affection."

My pastor has a saying that I absolutely hold near and dear to my heart, "You teach what you know, but you produce what you are." This leads me to believe that we as adults, first, must get out of our little boxes and explore spirituality for ourselves. You cannot have something withdrawn from you that isn't there to begin with. As much as I would like to go to the ATM and withdraw thousands of dollars out, I can't. This is because it isn't in there. The same goes for spirituality. I can't display spirituality if I am not a spiritual person. It gives me a sense of responsibility and great humility when my friends come to me for spiritual advice. To hear the words, "You are the only person I felt comfortable talking to about this", makes me feel as if I am exuding a spirit led life. Sure, I joke and act silly, and "keep it real", but they know I will give them sound spiritual advice about various aspects of their respective lives when the need arises. If more of our young black men had more men in their life that they could do this with they would not get bad advice or act out of frustration, leading to something detrimental. I truly believe that many of our young black men find themselves in bad situations simply because they did not have anyone to reason with, spiritually. For so long our young men have been taught to combat everything physically. In some cases there is nothing wrong with that. Men have to learn to defend themselves, their property, and their loved ones. We are going to be rough around the edges at times. That is our makeup. However, we also have to teach them the value of being spiritually fit as well. Spirituality does not denote weakness. Being a spiritual person quite possibly could be the greatest sign of strength it is.

5

The Value of Self

"A mirror is not for admiration...but for correction."

I distinctly remember reading three words that literally changed my life, "Know Thy Self." It hit me like a ton of bricks. It stuck to my spirit, and I have lived by those three words to this day, so much so to the point where it was my first tattoo; inked on my right arm. Knowledge of self, though commonly linked to Five Percenter beliefs (a spin-off of the Nation of Islam), is probably the key ingredient to one's personal fulfillment. The first book I had ever planned on writing (and probably still will), was/is going to be entitled, "The Young Black Male Identity Crisis."

I truly believe that since slavery, we as black men have had problems valuing ourselves. We often, as many in all races do, put our value in material things to try and cover up what we lack in self-love and self-identity. This chapter will cover many areas and hopefully conclude the point I am trying to make with this entire book...loving your face. It seems as though black men have been subliminally taught to hate ourselves, be ashamed of who/what we are, and ultimately, settle for being less than or second class. We have overcome great obstacles in the past, and we have no reason to stop now.

Hopefully, this chapter will analyze where we are as black men, where we have come from, and more importantly, how positive self-identity will create the pathway to where we are going.

Writer's Block (An Awakening)

Usually if I get a concept I can write on it for days on end. However, with this particular chapter of the book, I probably went through the worst writer's block I had ever experienced. I would take my manuscript to work and try to write on my break. I came up with nothing. I would come home after work and try to write. I came up with nothing. I would cancel studio sessions on Saturdays to solely focus on finishing this chapter. Again, I came up with nothing. Some of my friends who helped me throughout the process of the book would always ask me how the book was going. I would tell them about my writer's block and they would look confused. These are the friends who were as equally excited about me finishing the book as I was. I considered abandoning the whole idea of the book because I knew that this chapter would summarize the whole concept of Hate My Face. *"Perhaps this is God telling me that this book is not a good idea"*, I thought. I was perplexed, frustrated, and angry. For the life of me I could not figure out why I couldn't finish this chapter. Other chapters I could write 3-4 pages worth of material a night...but with this chapter; absolutely nothing. I finally decided to seek God because I knew there was a deeper meaning behind this dilemma and not just happenstance. I got this revelation. I cannot write on something that I am not able to relate to. Like a ton of bricks it hit me. I was trying to write on issue that I struggled with myself. It would be the equivalent of me writing a cookbook on French cuisine, repairing a water heater, speaking Mandarin, or some other element/trade I was not skilled in. Thanks be to God, however, the writer's block broke. After much self-evaluation, life changing events including the death of one my grandmothers, and several life lessons, I present to you, The Value of Self.

Facing The Reality of You

"Lil' Man, Lil' Jr., Shorty, Lil' Chuck, Lil' Dude..." you name it: I have been called them all.

Hate My Face

At the age of 32 years old, I stand a mere 5 feet 6 inches tall, topping out at right around 160 lbs. My peak weight to this day has been 165 lbs. I have always been the "little guy." My dreams of being a star running back for the Pittsburgh Steelers quickly died after having the wind knocked completely out of me while running a play on a kickoff return when I played Jr. varsity football in the 9th grade. I decided that I was better off sticking to the marching band. I was simply not big enough to be a contact sport athlete. Sure I had heart, but weighing a mere 88 pounds my 9th grade year and trying to be a star wingback simply was not smart. I can look back on that now and laugh.

    The reason I mentioned that is because, back then, I had the wrong idea about what I wanted to become. I think most every boy, at least once in their life, has dreams of being an athlete. They want to be the next Michael Jordan, Emmitt Smith, or Barry Bonds. I had always been a lover of music but because all of my friends wanted to be athletes, thus I wanted to be one. As time progressed and I being to dive deeper into music and writing, I realized that I was destined to exercise my God given talents through a pen and an instrument. It was not until I came into my own that I figured out that my calling was in arts and not sports.

It dawned on me at that moment that was okay not to fit in. I was different. I was in middle and high school listening to classic jazz, constructing songs in my head and then going home to try to interpret them on my 32 key Casio keyboard. I learned who I was as far as my gifting was concerned.

However, even to this day, I still struggle with who Charles is. Sure, I am a writer, poet, musician, etc…but I still sometimes deal with ME. A person can be identified by what they do. When we think of Ving Rhames or Denzel Washington, we automatically think "actor." When we think of Jay Z or Diddy, we instantly think "entertainer, mogul." When we think of Hines Ward (shout out to the Pittsburgh Steelers), Chris Paul, or Tiger Woods, we think "athlete."

These are the things that define these individuals on a surface basis. This is how they are defined by society.

Let's look at this from another angle. Up until 1994, everybody looked at O.J. Simpson as a former star NFL running back (easily in my top 5 greatest running backs in history). He was a revered and highly respected athlete in the Hall of Fame of sports. However, after 1994, nobody really ever looks at O.J. Simpson as just *that person* anymore. Some people tend to look at him as a murdering wife abuser. As a result of the high profile murder case, the press, the books, the endless media coverage of this tragic event, and the slandering, we now look at him as another person in a sense.

The same can go for Kobe Bryant, Michael Vick, and many other high profile celebrities who have "fallen from grace." As a result of unfortunate circumstances, a new layer of these individuals was exposed to the public. The shell of their "representative" was peeled off and we saw THEM. Keep in mind; I am not screaming guilt on these individuals at all. OJ was found innocent, Kobe was found innocent, R. Kelly was found innocent, so I will stick with the verdict of the courts for the sake of the book and the point I am aiming for. My point is, they were stripped of their shields and were forced to hand the media, their peers, and society a "mirror." Everywhere they looked, they had to deal with themselves.

I, myself, happen to be a fan of all of these individuals as it relates to their careers. I think that Kobe Bryant is one of the most electrifying and gifted basketball players to ever play the game. Michael Vick, in my opinion, was headed down the road to being named one of the NFL's greatest quarterbacks ever. R. Kelly, even in all of his musical antics, is by far one of the most innovative artists, songwriter and producer in music. I have a great respect for them all. They are proof that black men are some of the most gifted people on the planet. You cannot take this away from them. No matter what you heard, saw or witnessed, they had God- given abilities that no one can deny.

Hate My Face

The problem comes in when a person can no longer rely on his or her gifts and talents to be the litmus test for their true self.

Here's an example.

I recall speaking/performing in front of an audience full of women. My particular job that night was to "woo" them with poetry about love and relationship. This had to be by far, one of the best performances I had ever given. The microphone was nice and clear. The music was laid back and soothing. The glow from the candles in the dark room was hitting at all the right angles. Usually when I perform, I tend to do so with my eyes closed. It's as if I feel what I am saying more. I will admit, I was "feeling myself" that night. The vibe was nearly perfect. After about the third or fourth piece, I paused. I looked around the room and saw a myriad of dreamy eyed women of both races (black and white) who were enthralled and captivated by my words. You could hear a pin drop on soft cotton.

The music stopped. My voice went from "Barry White" to my regular speaking voice. I told them to not be fooled. I am not always this sweet. I do not sound like this all the time. I yell, I argue, I throw adult fits, I get immature, at times I do not want reason, and lastly, I am human.

I brought the women, and myself, back to reality. I, willingly, stripped myself of my gift and exposed *me*. After I said that, the vibe changed. I was no longer Superman Lover. I had come back to Earth from my journey to Planet Love. Instantly, I was no longer S.I.L.E.N.T.W.A.R. the poet, I was merely Chuck, the average guy. Granted, I tend to view myself as an extremely mild mannered, soft spoken, easy to get along with type of dude. However, I am not like that AT ALL TIMES.

I believe that often times we tend to live our life as the person we dream about being, and not as the person we actually are. This is why you see people in debt up to their eyeballs, buying something that the person *in their dreams* can afford with ease. They are purchasing their fantasies on credit and leaving their "reality" indebted to a false fulfillment. I look back now I reminisce about all the things I purchased *then* that are hindering me from buying a house *now*. It's sad that probably more than three-fourths of these things I cannot even name or no longer even have. These things are but a memory. However, I still have me, as well as my issues.

I am struggling now as a result of trying to be the man I deemed "had it all." Even if I were to become that man I dreamed about; if I still don't deal with "me", it is all for naught.

We have seen countless stories of people - celebrities who seemed to have everything going for them commit suicide. Why? They never dealt with themselves or their issues.

Countless movie stars, musicians, and millionaires have died as a result of drug overdoses. Why? They had become the people they dreamed about being, but never dealt with the person that they *are or were*.

Let me expound on this a little more.

When I say "me" I am not talking about merely me as a black man, I am speaking more about me as an individual. I am referring to the inner person who makes up my character. This includes my flaws, my demons, my fears, my passions, my faults, and my gifts. You can put yourself in this scenario as well.

If I have a fear of being rejected as a result of my childhood then no amount of money, jewelry or materialistic accumulation is going to change that. If a woman has trust issues with men then she can marry a billionaire and be divorced within a year. His fortune will not change that. It may cover it, but eventually her "issue" will override the fantasy. This is why you see the "Liz Taylor" effect in Hollywood. Issues were not dealt with.

Let's look at Michael Jackson and his dilemma. I honestly do not believe that Michael had any sexual dealings with those little boys. That is my opinion. I feel that the reason that Michael took such an interest in hanging around young boys (not saying that it was acceptable) was because Michael was trying to live out a childhood *he* was denied. Michael never really had a chance to be a kid in a sense. This is why he had the Neverland Ranch, pet monkeys, etc. He amassed all this wealth, had plastic surgery after plastic surgery, and won award after award. However, his issue of never being able to do things that average little boys did was never dealt with. I think he was never fulfilled. As a result, he tried to live out his fantasy way too late in his life, and his reality is paying the debt through slander and lawsuits. Simply put, I feel Michael never really had a chance to be *himself*.

The reason I used Michael as an example is because he is, as far as music is concerned, the black man that is probably the most synonymous with success on a worldwide scale. I will venture to say that the majority of mankind knows of this man in some form or fashion. He is, more than likely, the closest example of "having it all."

I truly believe that once a person makes an earnest decision to deal with them "inner evolution" takes shape.

One of the greatest examples of this, I feel, is R&B singer Mary J. Blige. I have long been a fan of Mary, from "What's The 411" to her latest releases. She cleverly did this through her music, and is one of the few artists who have successfully done so. If a person were to listen to her catalogue you can see the changes that took place in her life. She, unashamedly, did this through art. Her album titles alone speak volumes: "My Life", "Share My World", "Love and Life", "No More Drama", and, "The Breakthrough", to name a few. Mary dealt with her issues musically and brought forth a healing to herself and countless others. This is not to say that Mary does not presently deal with issues. Being a very successful artist, entertainer, and legend in her own time has to come with many hardships. However, I think through her music and self-exposure, she has learned how to cope better over time.

Staying in the musical vein, I have to mention one of my personal favorites, Tupac Shakur. Many people look at me funny when I mention him as one of my favorite artists in history considering my personal stance on the state of hip-hop. I have always said, and will continue to say that Tupac was a prophet who simply missed his calling. The enemy cut his life short, just as he did Martin Luther King, Jr., Malcolm X, and many others. Tupac, I feel, was one of the few artists that eloquently spoke of both sides of him (good and evil). We all have a good and evil side whether or not we want to admit it. He pinned lyrics so vividly and ahead of their time that they still touch me to this very day…deeply. He spoke of his demons, his angels, his passions, his hates, his loves, his self-destructive side, and also the side that loves life. The reason why Tupac is so revered now in the musical world is because he was transparent. He pulled no punches, put on no facades, he admitted when he was wrong, he sounded the alarm when government and society raped his people, and he spoke the things that most young black men felt internally. Tupac was the voice of every black man: the intellect, the street dude, the intellectual street dude, the gangster, the struggling father, the dope dealer who wanted a new line of work, the gang banger who had no father, etc. He was the personification, I think, of poetic and musical multi-dimensionalism.

To put it simply, Tupac, as Mary was/is, human. I remember the day I was sitting in the front room and saw it when Tupac's date of birth and date of death was surrounding a dash. I cried. I felt like my brother had died.

In fact, I think a lot of black men felt as I did. Tupac was that guy who would say things that a lot of brothers didn't have the guts to say or simply do not know how to say. He was a mouthpiece for the speechless in a sense.

I believe that when a person develops the characteristic of "realness," they are more at peace with themselves, be it good, bad or indifferent. However, this does not mean that they shouldn't change some things that are "real" about them. It seems that in today's society realness is sadly synonymous with machismo in the eyes of young black men. When someone truly "keeps it real", limitations are subconsciously put on the "it" portion of the phrase. If a person says that he will kill another brother over stealing money, he may, in some circles, be considered keeping it real. However, if that brother says that he will let God deal with that person and believe that his reciprocity will come through the fact that he forgives that brother and not retaliate, he very well may be considered a punk. In both instances, he was "keeping it real." In one sense, the brother was keeping it real on the strength of what the majority thinks should be done. On the other hand, the brother was keeping it real on what he fell would be best for his future, and simply making a sound and logical decision to not retaliate.

This all correlates with knowing "you." A man who admits he has a problem with lusting after young children is keeping it real with himself. Of course, we know that this is not right, however, admitting that is a start. If that particular man takes no initiative to get help, keeping it real was not enough. Once someone acknowledges that they have an issue that is detrimental to their future or the wellbeing of others, ie, alcoholism, drug abuse, domestic violence, habitual lying, stealing, and gambling, yet never does anything about it, they are merely making confessions without a lesson. In a lot of cases, lessons are not learned until that person inhabits a prison, homelessness, loneliness, or possibly a grave.

I am a prime example of this. I have suffered from depression for a great deal of my life but never quite knew what it was until my latter years. As a child, I distinctly remember getting down about the smallest things. I thought it was normal until I began to read up on depression symptoms. For quite some time I was ashamed of my condition until I realized that I could help other people who dealt with it as well but did not know.

I was in the sixth grade when I realized the something was abnormal about my moods. I remember there was a girl in my class (whose name I still remember) that was evidently poor and less fortunate. My classmates would make fun of her but I never did. I would go home and literally cry for her. I went into a depression for several weeks concerning her and nobody ever knew. At the time, I did not know that it was depression I was dealing with. I simply knew that it was different. It seems that after that I would always go into some type of depression several times throughout the year consistently, even to this day. I would constantly worry about something, be it minimal or grand.

I have since sought counseling from time to time and have learned to cope with my condition. I realize that, in the grand scheme of things, it makes me a stronger individual. It makes me appreciate life more.

Black Men and Historical Depression

I guess that my previous section is an excellent segue into this one. I can say that I was pretty blessed to have a black male psychiatrist that treated me. He was a real brother to the fullest extent. We instantly connected. He would always ask me how my music and poetry writing was going. For a while I had completely stopped doing both during the worst stages of my illness. He always stayed on me about sticking with those, as they were a major therapy for me. One of the things I can say that I most appreciated about him was that he met me exactly where I was as far as being a black man. He emphasized to never be ashamed of what I had to go through. The statement he made that stuck out to me was that there are millions of black men who suffer from depression and do not realize it. There are some black men who do or did suffer from depression that maybe we didn't know about.

Hands down, my most influential musical hero is Donny Hathaway. As many may or may not know, Donny Hathaway suffered from depression. I recall watching a special on Donny one day where some of his close friends were recollecting on the last few years of his life. One of his friends recalled a time in the studio where Donny had a "moment." He explained how Donny was doing a session and screamed to the top of his lungs and ran out of the studio in sheer terror. There were no obvious triggers present. The friend stated that he found Donny hiding in a room in utter panic. He said something that really made me think about black men and how it relates to depression. He said he asked Donny what was wrong. Donny replied (though in a state of hallucination) that white people had hooked machines up to his brain and were trying to steal his music. It stopped me in my tracks. It made me think about how even though Donny was suffering with schizophrenia; his fear was that a white person was oppressing him.

Ironically, Webster's dictionary defines being depressed as "being sad, dejected or reduced in degree and value." Black people are the deceptive epitome of this definition, historically speaking, even in its inaccuracy.

Black men are one of the most oppressed humans on Earth. During slavery we had to endure the humiliation of being beaten and demeaned in front of our wives and children, and simultaneously still had to be "leaders." I have always believed that we as black men suffer from a "historical" depression that we are not outwardly aware of, but are subconsciously aware of constantly. I believe that this goes further than having a slave mentality. This leans more so to still feeling the *mental* pain and anguish of slavery. Imagine wondering how certain white people really feel about you even you see, and interact with these people on a daily basis. When you walk into a store and you are the only black male in there, you sometimes sense the fear or hatred coming from other races of people. I'm not saying that this is the scenario every single time we are put in this situation, but sometimes it is present psychologically. There are triggers. There are certain words that my black friends can say to me that my white friends can't. It's an unspoken agreement.

Here's an example. One of my best friends, Lem, can call me "boy" all day. When we dap each other up it's usually followed by, "What up boy?" It's a black man's term of endearment. We, collectively, understand the phrase or greeting. I ran into an old friend of mine at church a few Sundays ago that I hadn't seen in probably 15 years. That same greeting was exchanged by both of us, along with a hug. I didn't flinch when he said it, and vice versa. Black men have a language we speak that some white people can't speak, even if they do not have an ounce of racism in their being.

On the flip side, one of my white friends, Alex, won't call me "boy." However, if he did, because we are that cool, I wouldn't say anything; but I know that Alex understands it would probably bother me. That is an invisible line not to be crossed. There is no doubt in my mind that Alex likes and respects me just as much as he does his other friends, but because there is an obvious difference outwardly, as far as race, there are some things, inwardly, that we have to respect as an unspoken code of conduct. I have often heard some brothers say that they have white friends that call them "boy", or even "nigga", and it doesn't bother them. I, honestly, find that very hard to believe. This may indeed be true. However, they must have reached some level of a kindred spirit that I may not have reached with Alex yet. I still consider him to be a true friend. Alex and I share a genuine love for music. He has heard several of my more "pro-black" records and liked them. We have discussed our collective relationship issues about our girlfriends from time to time. He has hung out at my apartment. When our job sent us to Miami, we hailed cabs together and hung out on South Beach and had a blast. That's my man. We click. I would have his back just as I would any of my black friends.

I said all that to say this. I'm not sure that if the day Alex and I were to get into a heated disagreement, and he calls me "boy", or "nigga" (which I honestly do not think he ever will), I would look at him the same way. Something inside of me would instantly lead me to believe that he has always looked at me as that. It changes the whole dynamic of the friendship, if there remains to be one.

When a black man calls another black man "boy", he probably has some sort of role in his life such as father, big brother, uncle, older cousin, close friend, and mentor. My father, to this day, periodically calls me boy when he wants to get my attention, or drive home a point. It's almost the black man's way of introducing a life lesson in a sense.

For example, my father would have probably said this to me had I told him I thought about abandoning the idea of this book. "Listen to me *boy*. "You better finish that book. Don't worry about what people have to say." It would have gotten my attention in a respectable way. I would have known he wasn't playing. I know that my father respects me as a man...simply because he raised me to be one. Respect is not the issue. He is still my father at the end of the day, and no matter how old I get, my father can tell me something once that a million other people have told me. It just sounds different coming from him. His voice holds power and authority in my life.

On the flip side of that, when a white man calls a black man "boy", it subliminally denotes superiority in *our* minds. It doesn't matter if they are joking. We wouldn't see it that way. It's embedded in us. Possibly if a black man, for whatever reason, was raised by a white man, be it a stepfather from birth or whatever, it may be different. For the most part that isn't the case. I honestly believe that in the back of our minds, somewhere deep in the recesses of our psyche, it takes us back to slavery, or segregation times. It's an instant flashback in a sense.

I think back to the 2008 presidential debate when Senator John McCain referred to Senator Barack Obama, as "that one." It bothered *us* as black men specifically. I thank God that it was Barack running and not my father. I think the debate may have ended a tad early that night. Having a kindred spirit with now President Obama, it made us feel that Senator McCain was lowering all of us to level of inferiority to where our name wasn't even worthy to be called. I'm sure that President Obama, even with the huge amount of dignity, class, and integrity that we have all grown to love him for, felt a little sting from that comment. This takes nothing away from his/our self-confidence, but a trigger is a trigger nonetheless.

Quite possibly, had we never been slaves or considered three-fifths of a human at one point in history, these statements probably wouldn't bother us. However, because we had this etched into our psyche for so long that this was true, even after coming into the knowledge that it wasn't, it stills bothers us when it is spoken.

This case has its positives and negatives. Both, however, I feel causes a certain amount of stress and depression on the black man. In the positive sense, a black man can take these types of statements/stereotypes, etc. and be driven to strive harder in life to achieve goals and progress to make sure he is the exact antithesis of what history has to deemed him to be. This, however, will cause him to work harder, be put into situations where he may have "submit" to someone of another ethnicity in order to climb a ladder while trying to maintain a certain amount of racial integrity. This causes stress and depression. It could start as early as grade school. It may not even be known to that man that this is what he is dealing with, and it could be the root of another depression that is more prevalent. I think in the situation with the young lady in my middle school, I could possibly not have wanted her to experience a pain that my ancestors have felt, including being laughed at, picked on, underprivileged, and poor. It could have been that I noticed a pain in her that, historically, I could relate to. Inevitably, because it was not dealt with then, it led to a repetitive process. I may be wrong, but if you really think about it, it makes sense. It all ultimately leads to different types of depression.

The other scenario is when a black man sees this obstacle and chooses to accept it. He accepts that he is inferior and spends his entire life with a victim mentality. One thing that my father has always said to me was that life doesn't owe me anything. Once you have life itself, life has done its job. It is up to you what decisions you make and what paths you choose to follow. I feel that a great majority of black men simply just do not care. This is not good at all. What's worse is that it has been adopted as a justifiable excuse for failure. I know in my case, and certainly probably many more black men, I had come to a point in my life where I simply did not care anymore. Thankfully, I grew out of that stage quickly when I began to acquire knowledge of self-worth and the power of determination.

Hate My Face

One of the worst things for anybody to do is to get to a point in life where they do not care, and never grow out of that stage. This is far worse when that person has responsibilities such as children.

I honestly believe that in certain cases this is a not a conscious decision that a man makes. When a man lives a life of relative honesty, goes to work everyday, abides by the laws of the land, and still comes up short at the end of the day, he may take a downward spiral into this mindset. I read an interesting statement that said, *"When a black man doesn't feel he can provide for his family or protect his children, he feels worthless and may in end up turning on another black man. Society seems to only value what you do and not who you are."*

I would imagine that he has to do something that seemingly will validate what little manhood he perceives he has left. The effects of this can lead to drug dealing, robbing, thievery, and other things.

Studies show that the average black man who commits suicide is less than 25 years old. Ironically, studies also show that white men generally commit suicide over the age of 40. Interestingly enough, the studies say that the reason why most black men commit suicide at such young ages is because they have simply lost hope. They said the reason why the majority of white men who commit suicide later in life do so is because they realized they have achieved many things: wealth, power, status, corporate respect, and future financial security, yet realize there are left internally unfulfilled. A black man's dilemma is much different. Everything seems to be against them: society, the justice system, and the employment system. Most black men can tell you that, at some point in their life, they realized that it is hard to be a black man. It is difficult to maintain integrity when you know that, behind closed doors or blatantly, you are being stereotyped. It is hard to know that if something gets "stolen" from the workplace, or suspiciously comes up missing that you are going to be the prime suspect, even in the midst of your innocence. At times we want to lash out and "go shell" due to the injustice we deal with. Yet, we can't. We have to live. We have to eat. We have to provide for our families.

I, in no way, condone drug dealing or any illegal lifestyle. Let me clear that up. However, I will say this. Probably, a great majority of black men that do this did not wake up one morning and decide that wanted to slang dope for a living. Some of the guys I know that were once involved in that lifestyle said that was their last option. Putting in job applications was not feeding their children. Going on interviews and being declined a position was not keeping their heat on and keeping their rent paid. Being denied government assistance was not keeping gas in their car or giving them bus fare to make it to the next interview, only to be rejected. Even though it a dangerous and frivolous lifestyle, they were not judged by their counterparts. They make their own hours. There was not the fear of being "fired" for no reason. They were their own bosses in a sense. They were not laughed at because it was evident that they barely stayed in compliance with the dress code. They made their own rules. There was no mandatory overtime. There were no yearly evaluations. They set their own salary depending on the strength of their hustle, and not because of education or the lack thereof. Lastly, in some sort of strange way, they felt respected.

Granted, these things do not make this sort of lifestyle acceptable, but it has to be put into consideration. I know several guys I grew up with that did these things and had a heart of gold. However, they were at the end of their rope. They felt hopeless.

I said all of that to say this.

Every man has to come into the knowledge of their wrong for themselves. There has to be that moment of clarity where they wake up and realize that changes have to be made. This all coincides with knowing "you" and realizing that you are better than your current situation, or choices that you have made. If a man was once involved in this type of lifestyle and never got caught, he will tell you that one day he realized he had to make a change. I honestly do not believe that no one wants to purposely live a villainous existence forever. I was listening to a friend of mine recite a rhyme about being remorseful for his days of slinging dope. In a very powerful verse he said, "I served one lady and found out it was my man's momma...forgive me momma." At that point he realized he was the embodiment of his brother whom he was selling his mother crack to. That is powerful. It dawned on him that it could have been his mother purchasing the poison. Instantly, right there on that block, he had a moment of clarity. True enough, not all brothers will have this moment. I have known some brothers whose mother is their biggest client. It's sad. Here again, we have to realize that the world is comprised of good and evil.

However, for those brothers who do indeed experience this moment, the inner revolution begins.

A Special Ed-ucation (The Verse)

We have all learned in school about George Washington Carver, Charles Drew, and other black inventors and intelligentsia. I read an interesting fact that stated there were several other inventions and creations that black men were responsible for but were denied patents. Thus, white men took the credit. Black men are genius. We are the most copied people on the face of the earth. Elvis Presley stole Chuck Berry's style and was deemed the king of rock and roll. I could go on and on. It is a rather touchy subject for me thus I will leave it alone and not stray away from the intent of this section.

    I guess this is why I have such a problem with a great majority of hip-hop. It gives a warped perception to our kids that being illegal and treacherous defines success for black men. It does not show the beauty in us. It does not show the character of us in a positive light. It defiles the precision and care that was given in our creation. It poisons the purity in our creative process, and allows us to partake in selfishness for the sake of a dollar. Crack takes the place of gifted hands, and a gun replaces cleverness in times of quick thinking.

Legendary rapper Special ED put it like this in the classic joint Crooklyn, *"Panic, as another manic depressant adolescent stares at death...now what's left when there ain't no guide and a whole lot of pride? It might be a homicide, so let the drama...slide."* This is one of my favorite opening lines of all the thousands of hip-hop songs I have heard. It makes such a powerful statement. I will attempt to break this down as I did rhymes in previous chapters.

"Panic, as another manic depressant adolescent stares at death." Here I think Ed is saying that there is a panic (nationwide, hood wide) whenever trouble brews for an adolescent. We all feel this. Not only does he say adolescent, he describes the type of adolescent...manic depressant. The derivative of the word manic is *mania*. Webster's dictionary defines the word mania, in one sense, as a strong, ungoverned, and desirable craze. The word

depressant I think is used in the same light as the word depressive, but was altered for the sake of the rhyme scheme. The word depressive means low in spirit, down, or low in vitality. If we put this together, we see a young man who is manically depressed. His depression is overwhelming in high gear, his thoughts are unclear. He is being energized, in a sense, with lowliness...AS AN ADOLESCENT. On top of all of this, he is staring at death. I am going to assume that Ed didn't mean at a certain place or time, as in that moment he was possibly staring down the barrel of a gun. Being that the song was about life growing up in Brooklyn, I will assume that he was speaking in general about the day to day possibilities of losing your life growing up in this environment.

"Now what's left, when there aint no guide and a whole of pride..." Here Ed asks a very potent question. What does this kid have left when there is no guide? Guide can take on a lot of meanings...spiritual guide, father, father like figure, God, mentor, etc. He is stressing the importance of having a person to look up to and hold you

accountable. What's left when this is non-existent? Wow. Then he adds another important element to the rhyme equation..."*And a whole lot of pride.*" Pride, as stated in the Bible is one of the seven deadly sins, amongst the things that God hates. Pride is defined as arrogance, conceitedness, and with this verse I think Ed is defining pride as being not being teachable. He is not heeding to wisdom. Nobody can tell this kid anything. So here we have an adolescent who is soaking in depression due to his surroundings, is staring at death on a daily basis, which has no sort of guide, and is also prideful (will not listen). Keep in mind, that this is just a few lines of ONE verse. This represents the power of words. What does this lead to? *"It might be a homicide."* When a young man does not listen, is full of pride, is manically depressed (he is letting his depression be transformed into hardness or gangsterism), and has no guide...he may be getting closer to death (homicide.) Then Ed makes a final plea, *"So, (please) let the drama...slide."*

When we think about the fact that this could be the scenario for millions of young black men, we have a serious problem.

The reason why I chose to break down that particular verse is because of the powerful point that it makes.

It's warning that Ed is making very clear. We have a problem that needs to be addressed, not only in Brooklyn, but nationwide. Without black men being in touch with their true spiritual identity, panic is inevitable.

Leaving the Past Behind

Besides Jesus, I would have to say that my favorite person in the Bible was King David. Why? He kept it real…with himself and God. In Psalm 31: 9-10 David says this, *"Have mercy upon me, O Lord, for I am in trouble. Mine eye is consumed with grief, yea, my soul and my belly. For my life is spent with grief, and my years with sighing: my strength faileth because of mine iniquity, and my bones are consumed."*

Hate My Face

Here we see that, obviously, David is expressing deep inner turmoil. He clearly states that he is in trouble, full of grief (mentioned twice), is lacking strength (weak), and is simply hurting (my years with sighing.) Any biblical scholar will tell you that King David was one of the most interesting people in the Bible. His life was chronicled from his famous incident with Goliath until his death. The thing that I liked and respected most about David was that he was not afraid to admit his failures.

If you notice in this passage of scripture David makes a very bold statement. He says, "My strength faileth because of MINE iniquity." Iniquity is defined as a wrongful or unjust act. We clearly see that David is plainly saying, "I am in this mess because of something I did wrong." If we continue to read on, David continues for the next few verses to speak of his pain, and his troubles. However, in verses 16-17, David gets his "swagger" back (to put in modern day terms.) He says this, "(16) Make thy face to shine upon thy servant: save me for thy mercies' sake. (17) LET ME NOT BE ASHAMED, O Lord; for I have called upon thee, let the wicked be ashamed. Let them be silent in the grave."

As I stated in a previous chapter, there could be years in between verses, so I am not quite sure how long this transformation took place. The more important part is that it (the transformation) did. If you notice in this passage of scripture, David never lost his identity. In the midst of all of his grief, sorrow, confession of wrongdoing, pain, remorse, and weakness, David never denounced his kingship. Why? He knew who he was and who God created him to be. In verse 14 he says, "I am forgotten *as* a dead man out of mind: I am a broken vessel." Notice that he never said he was a dead man, He said *as* a dead man. In essence what he is saying is that, "God, I *feel* dead." You can *feel* a certain way, but the reality is the direct opposite. Feelings never change the reality, but the reality changes the feelings.

The part of this passage that I absolutely love is the plea that David makes to God, "Let me not be ashamed." If you have not noticed by now, I am a firm believer in looking up the true definition of words. It can change the whole dynamic of a statement; especially when reading God's word. Let is defined as "to permit." If you are asking somebody to let you do something, you are actually asking for their permission. Here David is asking for God's permission to pass over the shame he is experiencing. He is saying, "God I have confessed my wrong to You; now permit me to get past it and continue reigning under Your authority." He never denounced his kingship. He realized that there were battles to be fought, people to lead, etc. and that he did not have time to wallow in his iniquity. That's powerful. He had to get past his past to make his vision of his future present tense.

    The point I am making is that a big, unspoken ailment amongst black men is the "shame" element. Some of us are ashamed of things we have done. We are ashamed of how we grew up. Many black men are bequeathed shame from their fathers. This is what I refer to as the "just like yo' daddy" syndrome. I lived a long time being ashamed of decisions/choices I made. One of my biggest shames was that I always felt like I never lived up to my biological father's standards as far as education. I often think that this is why he has chosen not to play a role in my life consistently. We are still dealing with the *feelings* of what we did or didn't do in the past, and not focusing on the *reality* of what we are, or what we can become. Prisons and juvenile institutions are full of prosecuted *leaders* who never quite learned the reality of who they are. This goes for the rapist, murderer and drug dealer. Regardless of how hideous a person's crime is, the reality of what they were created to be never changed.

When a person deals with a certain percentage of shame, accepting their God-given greatness is always hindered.

Let's deal with this issue of shame.

Webster's dictionary defines the word shame as: a painful feeling caused by a sense of guilt, unworthiness, impropriety (improperness), and disgrace. At some point in their lives, everyone deals with a certain amount of shame. Some are quick to get over it, and others are not. I fall in the latter category.

In Jeremiah 3: 24-25, the Bible says this, (24) *"For shame hath devoured the labour of our fathers from our youth; their flocks and their herds, their sons and daughters. (25) We lie down in our shame, and our confusion covereth us: for we have sinned against the Lord our God, we and our fathers, from our youth even unto this day, and have not obeyed the voice of our Lord."*

Let's get a clear understanding of what is going on. One of the key principles and purposes of the book of Jeremiah is to show the patience and love of God towards an unrepentant nation. So we see here that Jeremiah is calling for a people to turn from their disobedience and understand that God loves them.

If you notice that in this passage of scripture, the prophet Jeremiah says that "shame" has devoured all of things that these people's fathers have achieved since their youth. He made it clear that it was the shame that brought about this. It wasn't the actual things that caused the people to be ashamed, but only the shame of it. In other words, they were not able to get past it. They wallowed in it. Here we see that shame alone has devoured wealth, families, and a nation as a whole. I want this to sink in. It was the shame. The reason I firmly believe this is because in verse 25 Jeremiah says, [for we have sinned against the Lord *our* God.] In the latter portion of the verse he repeats himself by saying, [and we have not obeyed the voice of the Lord *our* God.] In this same verse Jeremiah makes an interesting statement, *"We lie down in our shame, and our confusion covereth us."* This leads me to believe that shame and confusion tie in together. Notice he didn't say that they lied down and was merely confused; he said that they lied down in their shame and confusion *covered* them. When something is covered, it is consumed by whatever is covering it. I will take a risk here and venture to say that the reason they were confused is because they were so bound by the bad choices, sins, etc. that took place, they possibly may have no longer realized their worth. They had become zombies; oblivious to the reality of redemption and God's promises. However, the whole time, Jeremiah seems to be saying that God is still *their* God. He is still claiming them as His children. Fellowship may have been broken, but not the covenant. I think that many young black men are constantly lying down in their shame and are covered with confusion. When a person is covered in confusion, you cannot possibly expect them to make rational decisions. Though many black men will not admit it, possibly due to pride, they exist with a mentality of shame. If they are not freed from that shame then they will continue to do shameful things because it is their mentality. They will have a hard time excepting praise simply because they are still covered in shame for something that they did a long time ago. When a convicted felon has served his time in prison and has made a conscious effort to turn around his life, yet not be eligible to vote, the laws of the land are still covering him in his shame. It's the government's way of saying, "You will continue to wear this scarlet letter even though you have served your debt to society." In essence, they have served their tangible sentence in prison, but must now also serve an intangible life sentence of shame by not being considered an equal citizen again. This, in my opinion, is one of the biggest morale killers amongst young black men. It's the equivalent of taking away a man's voice. If he can't vote, he cannot be heard.

In another scenario, when a young brother is constantly reminded of how sorry his father was/is by his mother or other family members, he is being covered by a recycled shame.

While many of these problems are not easily dealt with or shoved away, we have to remember that it is imperative for a young black man to understand that he is "meant to be." I believe that no one is placed on Earth by mistake. Granted, some die in their confusion, and some are just simply taken away by evil forces (crime, sickness, disease), but everybody is born with a purpose.

Hate My Face

The Obama Effect

<u>*Step Your Game Up: November 4, 2008*</u>

Collectively, our games were forced to step up...

Next up to the plate to create pathways for our families...is us.

Thank Barack.

Thank the Rock.

The reciprocity of Simon of Cyrene was seen on all our TV screens and the screams of "we can't do it" were instantly silenced.

Now the excuses are useless. The nooses we used to set for each other are now covered with Obama '08 stickers and posters...I can't leave you hanging no more, I have to hold you closer.

I have to hold you more accountable and encourage you to overcome that which is deemed insurmountable.

I need you to do the same, thus our destinies can be renamed...accomplished.
I'll tell you and you tell me to...
Step your game up.
Step your name up to being capitalized at all times from now on...we are forced to be proper nouns...
Now forced to drape our women in the most proper gowns...
No more "hand-me-downs", social and emotional letdowns, and discount consignment shop tiaras and crowns...
We epitomize kingship from this point on, no longer paupers now...we are rich.
Can bitch still be used to confuse our sons as the namesake of our first ladies?
Shall we still neglect our babies?
Will we now think twice before overlooking "Keisha" for "Katie?"

Hate My Face

Not racist by any means...but the scene of a shapely Michelle will fit so well when we tell our grandchildren that "our" first First Lady was a real "sista."

Let's get real mister...

Step your game up.

The whole dynamic of being a brother has now shifted. We have long been gifted...But now our consciousness has been lifted to another plateau...a different dimension...an elevated plane...Our brains now have a "priority" sticker placed on them...and our reality is no longer grim.

Thank Barack.

Thank the Rock.

The shanks and glocks that we used to destroy us should now implore us to think twice before they are used to take a life...A black one at that.

Shall we still rap about the fallacious machismo of a thug nigga, when decades ago they drug "niggas" away from the voting booths to cast of a ballot of truth, or shall the youth continue to harmonize ballads of drug niggas who "make it do what it do?"

Will Tony Montana be rightfully replaced by Barack Obama as our young men's vision of success?

Shall we still stress that dress is more important than clothing our son's minds with the knowledge of the time when we were seen as three-fifths of a gift?

Shall we still sift through life with dreams of reaching "baller" status, or will the apparatus of change rearrange our though pattern?

Shall we still settle for being seen as more hyper-sexual than intellectual?

Will we now stop exchanging monetary compensation for subliminal black-facing?

Shall we still glorify the pimpification of the black nation?

Will we still be trophy-casing our women as showpieces and not masterpieces, while the Master pieces together a creation of what the world thought to be a figment of blacks' imagination...A man running the White House with dark pigmentation?

Hate My Face

Now, my brother...I urge you to...

Step your game up.

He was the underdog too.

Step your game up.

A single mother raised him too.

Step your game up.

His father was nothing more than a stranger too.

Step your game up.

They dogged him to the dirt too.

Step your game up.

They tried to use his own race against him too.

Step your game up.

They called him a nigger too.

Step your game up.

He always kept his cool. Can you?

Step your game up.

I could imagine the nights where the inner fights sent him on flights where the heights of seeing common ground were seemingly impossible.

He remained steadfast...and the last was named first.

The last hearse carrying the dying morale of black men ran out of gas and was refueled with high octane, put in a different lane, and renamed the Midnight Train to the Promised Land.

Pay your fare and let's get there; brother.

Step your game up.

Thank Barack.

But more importantly, thank the Rock.

Philippians 4:13

We all remember it. I'm sure that everyone recalls exactly where they were when it happened. We all knew it was going to happen long before it manifested, but it was that very moment that we hold near and dear in our hearts. November 4, 2008, roughly around 10:30 pm, we knew. The blue states were picking up and covering the TV screens as we repeatedly heard, *"And Obama has won (enter state here.)"* Anchormen from CNN, MSNBC, and even FOX News knew that a black man was about to be the most powerful man in the world. It wasn't a specifically a black man rising though; it was more of a nation growing, except for the sad amount of bigots who just couldn't bear the image of a black man running the United States.

However, no matter how modest an African American is, or how "colorblind" they claim to be, this election was special to *us*. I will admit that I shed a few years upon hearing, "Barack Hussein Obama will be the 44th President of the United States of America." It was then I realized this is going to change some things for us as black men. Now granted, the world has millions of successful black men, but none of them can say that they are the Commander-In-Chief of the most powerful nation on Earth. This was big. This was the visible proof to the world that black men can achieve anything.

The man who had endured media attack after media attack, racial slur after racial slur, lie after lie, character defamation after character defamation, and cruel joke after cruel joke was about to call the shots nationally.

I guess I set my hopes a tad too high thinking that this was going to bring blacks and whites closer. In some ways it did. I was more so hoping that it would change the image of black men to America. Here again, in some ways it did. I was hoping that the naysayers would at least give President Obama a chance to prove himself. That's where my hopes were dashed. They didn't. The attacks were vicious from the gate. I watched in disbelief as Sean Hannity of Fox News did an entire special trying to somehow link Obama to terrorism or having terrorist ties. It was appalling. We are all familiar with Rush Limbaugh's attacks on the President, and some of those theories made me question Limbaugh's so called allegiance to his country. I often wonder if this were white male democrat that had won the election, would the attacks be this severe. I highly doubt it. They were calling Obama incompetent, and incapable of running a country amongst other derogatory things. To take it a step further, I feel like had Obama been a black male republican running for office, the attacks would have come from his own party just the same.

Hate My Face

My point is this; I honestly believe that it had nothing to do with Obama's party affiliation. Clearly the man is capable of doing the job. He came into a nationwide mess, and is doing his best to clean up what was bequeathed unto him. Rush Limbaugh made an interesting statement. He said, "I want Obama to fail as president." Of course, he tried to justify his statement, but what he is saying is pretty cut and dry. I think what is trying to say is that he wants the president to fail so he could be proven correct in his theories. This is sad. How can a man want his leader (whether or not he wants to admit or not, he is his leader) to fail? That is the equivalent of a child saying that he wants his parents to fail, or his teachers to fail. I know some people may disagree with me on this, but I feel like it wasn't as much as Limbaugh wanted a democrat president to fail. Subliminally, he wanted to see a Black President fail. I do not believe that had it been Hillary Clinton, John Edwards, Bill Richardson, Dennis Kucinich, Chris Dodd, or any other democratic candidate this would have been said. After former Secretary of State Colin Powell (a Republican I might add) voiced his support and backing of Barack Obama, Limbaugh's first comment was because "both were black." Keep in mind, this is just my opinion, but Limbaugh's statements seem to mirror my theory. What I am trying to say is that there are forces on this earth that simply does not want to see, or does really believe that a black man is conditioned to achieve success or prosperity on this scale. This is even when there is sufficient evidence that disproves that. It's a sad reality. We have to teach our young brothers to get past that and prosper as God intended.

As we, as African Americans, proudly displayed our Obama bumper stickers and t-shirts (which I have a few myself), we were filled with pride to see one of our own achieve such a historical feat. President Barack Obama has to be one of the most charismatic, intelligent, and family oriented men a lot of us know. Along with these great qualities, he is also our president. One would have thought that this would have helped the image of black men as a whole. Please do not misinterpret what I am saying. Barack Obama, by no means, is our savior. I merely thought that he would be the catalyst for the shifting of America's image of black men. This happened a little bit but not much.

After all of the celebrations, rallies, election parties, and once most of the Obama/Biden '08 posters were taken down; I was quickly brought back to reality. If a white person saw me as a nigger on November 3rd; November 4th did not change that. If another brother saw me as his enemy for some reason on November 2nd, November 4th did not change that. Granted, there were some wonderful things that came out of this election. There were some young black men that voted who had never voted before. There were other young black men who had never given a second thought to politics who found themselves glued to CNN, etc. I've heard about some young black men who considered a career in politics after Obama's rise to leadership from obscurity. I have even began to think harder about getting a long overdue degree now that

President Obama has put the call out for all Americans to get some sort of education post high school. These are all great things and I thank God for favor on Obama's life to have such an impact on young black men's life.

I can say that the element that impressed me the most about Barack Obama was his confidence.

He definitely "knew self."

He never crumbled under pressure. Why? He was confident in his abilities to run a country. He didn't let what others said about him move him. He handled so many situations with sheer grace, intellectualism, and elegance that it made many of us wonder if anything bothered him.

Amidst of all this, at the end of the day, Obama's election is not going to change much until a young man's inside is changed. President Barack Obama is proof that once a young black man knows self, he can do anything.

The Major "Minor" Factor

It seems as though society has conditioned black men to look at themselves as less valuable than other races.

Hate My Face

One of my biggest grievances with American culture is the term "minority." I have never liked this term. This is, however, the term dedicated to African-Americans; or anyone basically non-white. One day a few of my friends and I were talking in the studio and the subject of the word minority came up. Basically, I was saying that the root word of minority is "minor." I followed up by saying that anything labeled "minor" will not receive a lot of attention. For a minor cut or bruise you get a small bandage, and possibly a dab of alcohol, peroxide, or a typical ointment. For a major cut or bruise, one is rushed to the hospital. Few people know the homerun leader for Minor League baseball. The average American knows who Babe Ruth is. Hopefully you get my point by now. Anything that is minor is given little attention. I feel this applies to minority races as well, specifically African-Americans. I feel like there are many aspects of society that represent this. Have you ever noticed how terrible the conditions are in the projects in any city in America? Next time you drive in a low income area, take note of how bad the street conditions are. Then take a ride through the areas that the more privileged citizens live in. Go online and research the amount of black male students in behavioral classroom settings to that of white male students. If you ever visit Washington D.C, take a ride through the Georgetown University side of town, and then travel to the Howard University side of town. It's literally night and day. Moreover, do this in ANY city where there are both, an HBCU's (Historically Black College or University and a traditional college or University. You will see a vast difference. Ask any black male the amount of times he has stood in a line at a grocery store that is not on "his" side of town if he felt he was treated differently than the "other" customers. Ask him if he was greeted as politely as everyone else, if greeted at all. Folk labeled a minority will be treated as such. I never understood how "all men are created equal" yet a certain segment of the population is labeled the minority. It doesn't add it to me, and it is borderline oxymoronic.

Hate My Face

How Katrina Spoke To America

We all remember the tragedy of Hurricane Katrina. *(Even though I know Hurricane Katrina hit more places that New Orleans, I am choosing to solely focus on this city to get a point across.)* A great deal of New Orleans was flooded by this natural disaster. To add to that, a great deal of the lower income areas were literally swallowed by this storm. We are all well aware, and remember the inexcusable lack of response by the government to the Hurricane Katrina victims. There were non-profit organizations that arrived there to aid in helping victims even before the government did.

I find it not strange that New Orleans happened to be one of the poorest metropolitan areas in the United States. New Orleans also has a 70% black population; along with a black mayor, and great majority of it's political leaders being black as well.

It was said that members of the United States Congress said that the reason why relief efforts were delayed was because a great percentage of those affected were poor. Our, then, President George Bush even felt his vacation was more important than returning to Washington, D.C. the Monday the hurricane hit. He opted to return that Wednesday afternoon. Many people that know me know that I am a fan of Kanye West's music, but not of his blatant arrogance and off the wall antics. However, he said one of the most important things during this whole ordeal. Even though it was a bit uncouth; it shook up America, "George Bush does not care about black people." It needed to be said. I'm glad he said it. West verbally put a moral mirror to the face of American government and forced it to evaluate its self. I recall watching the media coverage of this disaster and seeing the endless footage of beautiful black people pleading for help, standing on rooftops, trapped in their homes, rowing in homemade boats on the flooded streets searching for refuge, little babies had lost their mothers to the streams, etc. It was a picture of black people in pain. In addition, Hurricane Katrina, in my opinion, was the personification of a great deal of African-

American male's emotional state. We are hurting. We are in pain. We feel hopeless. We are constantly wondering when our help will arrive. We act out in ways that are abnormal because we feel no one is paying attention to us. We will steal and loot during certain opportunities because "free" is a blessing to us, no matter how it comes to us. We are overlooked. We are abandoned. We are dying, and no one seems to care, and sadly we turn on each other as a result of our frustration.

The Value of Self

Self is defined as *one's own person known or considered as the subject of his own consciousness.* Whenever the word self is mentioned it will always means something in a singular sense. Nobody else is involved. If you ever notice, when somebody is acting strange, or is not acting as they usually do, the first thing someone says is, "He or she was not acting like himself or herself." They were instantly separated from their true character...their self.

Genesis 1:26 says, "And God, *"Let us make man in our image, after our own likeness, and let him have dominion..."*

The inherent character of God is love. Thus, if God said that all men were created in His image and likeness, then we are all born love-based people. Life, events, circumstances, and inherited traits corrupt this image. Moreover, at times, this can happen very quickly. I firmly believe that any person can be reverted back to this love-based existence. I also believe that only the love of Jesus can do this. Sure counseling, role models, good parenting, etc. can play a vital role, but only a spiritual reformation can solidify the change.

The root word of reformation is reform. To reform means to make morally better, to put an end to abuse or malpractice. Reform (another word) means to simply form again, as in re-form.

Simply put, it means to make something or someone again.

Many of our young black men need to be reformed, as well as re-formed.

I feel that reforming a person is an exterior process. Re-forming an individual is an inner change.

I think the greatest problem facing young black men are that they are not encouraged enough. They are not told how beautiful they are. Thus, one of the simplest ways to re-form a young man is building him up.

I feel like young black men are not praised enough…for the right things. An old saying goes, *"When I do ten good things; no one remembers. When I do one bad thing; no one forgets."* Young black men are constantly reminded of how much of a problem they are; so much to the point where it is accepted as normal. Just look at TV. Crime shows are mostly filled with imagery of young black men getting arrested, murdered or robbed. Hip-hop music seems to glorify the bad boy image of young black men.

Even though I know this is "meant" to be some sort of deterrent, it still lives a bad taste in the mouth of Americans towards young black men. It seems as though we have been made into a sort of villain to society.

I remember watching a special on TV where groups of 5 year olds were presented with a black baby doll and a white baby doll and asked which the bad one was. The overwhelming majority of the children picked the black baby doll as the bad, or the ugly one. This hurt me to my heart because all of the children were black themselves.

What is this saying? It is saying that, even at young ages, blacks seem to be taught that being black is not beautiful. They are being told, not necessarily through words, that dark skin is a setback. Malcolm X said that we are taught to hate black skin, black features and black blood. Those same features automatically become hateful to us. I am sure that the parents of these children are not teaching them that black skin is the equivalent of bad or ugly. However, the question is, are they being taught that it is, indeed, beautiful and a blessing? When our children are subliminally sent these messages about the negativity that coincides with being black; there has to some positive messages to counteract them. It is our responsibility as adults to drive these messages into our children.

God absolutely adores His children. He does not love the white man more than He loves the black man. He does not love the black man more than He does the white man. He loves us all equally. I have heard many people say that God does not see color. I disagree with that. I feel if that were the case then there would be no mention of ethnicity in the Bible. I also believe that everything happens for a reason. As it relates to the African American experience; I feel that there was a reason for slavery, and segregation. I do not know what that reason is. However, I do feel like that the once enslaved people will get reparations from God that no man, woman, child, law, or earthly force can stop from happening. I feel like the election of the first African American president was the beginning of it. I have always said this, and still believe it to this day, Simon of Cyrene, a Libyan (African) man who was specifically identified as being from Cyrene (modern day Libya) in the Bible, was not chosen to help Jesus bear the cross haphazardly. It was for a reason. Here again, I do not the specific reason, but I do feel like it holds a lot of weight. It has not been forgotten. An African man was the last person to assist Christ before His death for the salvation of mankind. While Simon of Cyrene has never been conclusively proven to be a black man; evidence shows that more than likely he was black considering his geographic background.

Why would I mention this? I mention this because I feel it is one of the true testaments that black men have purpose, a heart, and love for other people. Black men will go out of their way to help someone. It could be an elderly white woman at a grocery store who needs help carrying a bag of dog food, to another brother who is begging for spare change. We have heart. However, we have been so blasphemed and demeaned by society (and some by ourselves); it's hard to see beneath the surface. The mirror that the world has forced us to look into displays a manipulated image of an animal, an uncontrollable beast that does nothing but impregnate his women and leave the home, not having a job, drug dealing, murdering, and thieving creatures that lack substance. This is not us. This is not what God created us to be. More importantly, this is not how God sees us. God sees us as much His children as He sees those who do not bear this cross that we have to bear. He loves us just as much as He loves those who persecute us. God created us to look like Him. God did not create us to be carbon copies of each other, or carbon copies of the media depictions of us. God created us to have dominion. He gave us dominion over our responsibilities as fathers, husbands, and business men. The very face of God looks down on black men and smiles at us despite what society, and the world says about us. He looks past all of our faults, and sees Himself in us. Simply put, God has not forsaken black men. How could He? The image of the man that helped His Son bear the cross to Golgotha to die for the sins of the world cannot possibly be forgotten by God.

Our kingdom must be reclaimed. What is our kingdom? Our kingdom is anything that surrounds us. Our children are part of our kingdom. Our spouses are part of our kingdom. Our future is part of our kingdom. Our respect is part of our kingdom. Our health is a part of our kingdom. Our education is a part of our kingdom. Our pride in ourselves is part of our kingdom. Our heritage is part of our kingdom. Our gifts and talents are part of our kingdom. We have to stop letting others come in and rule our kingdoms for us. Imagine some man walking into your home. This man knows nothing about you, how you operate, your goals, your dreams, your family, or your life. He tells you that he will now control your house. He will dictate the financial routine. He will tell your son that he can achieve academically, and that he may get ahead through sports or music. He will tell your daughter that she is at the bottom of society's totem pole. He will tell her that she can only rely on looks or a nice body to get ahead. He will tell your wife how she should really view you according to the world's mirror. This is the equivalent of what is happening to us as black men. Our kingdoms are not our own anymore. We, sometimes unknowingly, allow these images, stereotypes, and stigmas control over our lives. We are forced to believe what the world says about us. Like a deer in the hot sands of the Kalahari, we go the river's edge to get a drink of water just to survive and end up in the mouth of societal crocodiles and eaten alive. Yet we continue to live, continue to go to that same river bank and hope that our thirst is quenched without incident.

Many of us, including myself, are bound by, or have been bound by fear. We have the tough exterior, that shell that everyone sees. However, when we to that quiet place where it's just God, us, and a mirror; we see failure. We see lack. We see defeat. We see our father's drug abuse, or alcoholism. We see our mothers dropping us off at grandmother's house when we were a child, and never returning. We see that little boy that misses his time with a father that not bothered to raise him. We see the molester. We see the disappointments of our life. We see the punishment we were given for crimes we had no knowledge of. We see guilt. We see the unforgiveness. We see pain. When will we start seeing the God in us? When we will see the clean slate that God has given us as a result of submitting ourselves to Him? When will we see the beauty? When will we see the very image of God smiling back at us? When will we see ourselves loving what we see? Make a choice today to no longer hate your face. Not necessarily your physical face, but the face of your future, the face of success, the face of the Love of God rooting for you in the midst of this race. I heard that today is God's way of saying, "Start over." Start today my brother.

Love your face.

Hate My Face

About The Author

Charles L. Crouch **(S.I.L.E.N.T.W.A.R.)** was born in Winston-Salem, NC in Jan.1976. Since his early childhood, Charles always had the knack for music, the arts, and writing. After performing in many talent shows and entering and winning various writing and poetry contests, Crouch discovered his passion; reaching people through words. It wasn't until the tragedies of September 11, 2001 when Crouch dove headfirst into a life of writing poetry. With a strong spiritual upbringing and always keeping in tune with the struggles, pains and triumphs of his people, Crouch began to receive local notoriety on the spoken word and hip-hop circuit. Eventually he became more exposed to the national scene through the Internet and an extensive travelling and performing schedule. Crouch has spoken and lectured at several universities across the country such as Winston-Salem State University, Southwest State University, Fisk University, The

University of Dayton in Ohio, The University of Mississippi for Women, and many more. Crouch has served as a counselor for at risk youth for several years. Crouch is regularly invited to speak at youth conferences, African American programs, hip-hop summits and spoken word venues. Armed with an extensive catalogue of poetry, songs, and miscellaneous writings, Crouch continues to grow as a catalyst for change and advancement for African American people and all mankind as a whole. He is currently pursuing his Bachelor's Degree in History, with a minor in Religious Studies. He is also the President and CEO of SpeakLife Enterprises and M.I.N.D.F.U.L.L. Music. Crouch, 36, currently resides in Raleigh, with his wife Lekisha. They have one son, Charles Jordan.

Hate My Face

For booking information please visit:

www.speaklifeenterprises.com or e-mail Charles at info@speaklifeenterprises.com

www.ingramcontent.com/pod-product-compliance
Lightning Source LLC
Chambersburg PA
CBHW032040090426
42744CB00004B/74